P9-CDK-308

Praise for

THE PERFECT YOU

"I now realize how exciting it is to live from my new heart. Everything in this new life flows from knowing 'the perfect you' and trusting Jesus within. In this captivating book, Andrew Farley and Tim Chalas invite you to celebrate God's perfect (and accurate!) view of you. You'll discover how to authentically live in God's grace and be freely inspired by the new, beautiful heart He gave you."

—BART MILLARD, singer/songwriter for MercyMe

"We're more than justified by faith. Believers in Jesus are regenerated, reborn, remade, and renewed by God's grace. It's high time we claimed our birthright. I am so grateful to Andrew Farley and Tim Chalas for bringing us back to the original, mind-blowing, heart-changing, relationship-restoring power of the Gospel!"

—BRUXY CAVEY, lead pastor of the Meeting House and bestselling author of *The End of Religion*

"Moralistic religion keeps yelling at you, 'You are and will always be bad, but if you love God, the least you could do is act good.' Buying into this system causes us to hide and live less authentically than before we believed in Jesus! In *The Perfect You*, Andrew Farley and Tim Chalas masterfully present a life-giving message of astonishing hope: Christ indwells you, and you are right on time. No bluffing needed. He adores you and is revealing the perfect you in His perfect way."

—JOHN LYNCH, renowned speaker and bestselling author of *On My Worst Day*

"I read a lot of books … once. It is rare when I read a book and think, 'I need to go back to this again.' Andrew Farley and Tim Chalas have given us a book that should be read at least once a year by every Christian. It's so easy to forget the biblical truths these guys have so beautifully described to us in *The Perfect You*. I'm an old guy who has just started thinking about his life in a different and exciting way. This book is a game-changer! Read it and you'll rise up and call Andrew and Tim blessed."

—STEVE BROWN, nationally syndicated radio host, seminary professor, author, and founder and president of Key Life Network

THE PERFECT YOU

THE PERFECT YOU

GOD'S INVITATION TO LIVE FROM THE HEART

ANDREW FARLEY
TIM CHALAS

SALEM
BOOKS
an imprint of Regnery Publishing
Washington, D.C.

Copyright © 2021 by Andrew Farley

All rights reserved. No part of this publication may be reproduced or transmitted in any form or by any means electronic or mechanical, including photocopy, recording, or any information storage and retrieval system now known or to be invented, without permission in writing from the publisher, except by a reviewer who wishes to quote brief passages in connection with a review written for inclusion in a magazine, newspaper, website, or broadcast.

Unless otherwise marked, all Scriptures are taken from the NEW AMERICAN STANDARD BIBLE®. Copyright © 1960, 1962, 1963, 1968, 1971, 1972, 1973, 1975, 1977, 1995 by the Lockman Foundation. Used by permission.

Scriptures marked NIV are taken from THE HOLY BIBLE, NEW INTERNA-TIONAL VERSION®. Copyright © 1973, 1978, 1984, 2011 by Biblica, Inc.™ Used by permission of Zondervan.

Scriptures marked NLT are taken from the HOLY BIBLE, NEW LIVING TRANS-LATION. Copyright © 1996, 2004, 2007 by Tyndale House Foundation. Used by permission of Tyndale House Publishers, Inc., Carol Stream, Illinois, 60188. All rights reserved.

The author is represented by Don Gates at The Gates Group, www.the-gatesgroup.com.

Salem Books™ is a trademark of Salem Communications Holding Corporation
Regnery® is a registered trademark of Salem Communications Holding Corporation

ISBN: 978-1-68451-127-3
eISBN: 978-1-68451-145-7

Library of Congress Control Number: 2020945143

Published in the United States by
Salem Books
An Imprint of Regnery Publishing
A Division of Salem Media Group
Washington, D.C.
www.SalemBooks.com

Manufactured in the United States of America

10 9 8 7 6 5 4 3 2 1

Books are available in quantity for promotional or premium use. For information on discounts and terms, please visit our website: www.SalemBooks.com.

To anyone who has ever questioned how good God is or how much He loves them, this book is for you.

(And by the way, that's all of us!)

CONTENTS

INTRODUCTION

You start your relationship with God, and everything seems amazing. But somewhere along the way—a month, a year, or a decade later—the magic fades away. The joy that first inspired you wears off. Frustration builds. Excitement dies. You find it again, briefly, at a particularly moving worship service, a retreat, or a moment alone with God in nature. But it never lasts. You end up asking: *What happened? Where did it all go? Is this all there is?*

Pretty soon, you conclude you have a wish list that just isn't going to be fulfilled on this side of Heaven. You want connection, consistency, closeness. But the more you wish for them, the further off they seem.

What's on your wish list?

__I wish my whole heart belonged to God.

__ I wish I looked more like Jesus on the inside.

__ I wish I were closer to God.

__ I wish I didn't want to sin so much.

__ I wish I were more dependent on God.

__ I wish I had more love for God.

Did you check one of these wishes? Two? Maybe most of them? Even all?

Don't worry—you're not alone. We all desire and seek after these things at one time or another. But here's the incredible news: *Because of Jesus, you already have them.* Yes, every single one of these wishes has *already* been granted.

"How can that be," you may ask, "if I don't feel any of it?"

We hear you. We feel the ups and downs of everyday living on the planet too. Like you, we also hear a good portion of the religious world saying the opposite: *You need to chase after these things all the days of your life—even if you don't seem to be making progress.*

But what if your feelings—often programmed by the opinions of others—are wrong on this one? Wouldn't that be worth knowing? As we walk through this book together, you're going to discover some powerful yet counterintuitive truths along the way. You'll learn that no matter what you might feel, these are 100 percent true of you:

- Your whole heart belongs to Him.
- You are as clean and as righteous and as holy as Jesus on the inside.
- You are as close to God as Jesus is—right now and forever.

- You don't really want to sin, and there's a shocking reason you still do.
- You are naturally dependent on God. It's actually your new default setting.
- You have an undying love for God. You don't need more love for Him.

THE COUNTERINTUITIVE TRUTH

Some of these may seem difficult to believe right now. They may run counter to what you've learned. These truths may contradict some of the books you've read and the messages you've heard. They may even seem to disagree with your own life experiences—your feelings and your failures. But as you'll discover in this book, they are indeed truths about you. And these truths are absolutely key to any genuinely fulfilling life in Jesus.

As you deepen your understanding of these radical truths, they will transform the way you approach life. No, this book will not fix your circumstances. It doesn't offer false promises of health or wealth or guaranteed success in your activities. That wasn't the early Church's experience, and it's not ours today.

What we promise to deliver in this book is a revelation of how you can enjoy a God-centered contentment despite your circumstances. If you decide to believe and act on what is written here, you will gain a never-ending, bone-deep assurance that you are okay no matter what. Here, we are not talking about okayness in the future or okayness in Heaven. We're not talking about okayness after a lengthy sanctification process or some heroic effort on your part.

No, we're talking about coming to know *the perfect you*—who you are right here and now, without any self-improvement. This book will put you on the path to seeing who you really are and give you the tools to see yourself and God in a whole new way. You'll gain a new awareness of your core passions and desires. You'll better understand what God did for you *and to you* when you believed in Jesus. And you'll learn to engage with others in new and practical ways as you accept God's invitation to live from your heart.

Think of this book as an introduction to your new spiritual heart and how to relate to God as He always intended. Here's the best part: It's great news all the way through. There's no fly in the ointment. There's no worm in the apple. There's no hidden agenda to get you to "do more" or "be more" for God. Quite the opposite! We want to show you just how new and perfectly beautiful God has *already* made you.

PART 1

IN SEARCH OF PERFECTION

CHAPTER 1

As we survey popular Christian messages these days, here are some of the main takeaways:

- You need to "spend more time" with God.
- You need to worship more.
- You need to prove your love for God.
- You need to slow down in life to be more spiritual.
- You need to rid yourself of all distractions.
- You need these strategies and steps to live better.
- You need to fast.
- You need to meditate.
- You need to hunger and thirst for more of God.

These incoming messages of "do more" and "be more" are shaping the most common flavors of Christianity today. And they're triggering an avalanche of worry, shame, and guilt. We start measuring ourselves by an ever-growing list of unrealistic religious standards. Soon we are taken hostage by them.

The message you eventually take in is this: *I am not enough.* The "strong Christian" model is verbally displayed for you nearly every Sunday. It's a Christian who does enough, who gives enough, and who is enough. It's the image you strive for. But you end up exhausted and frustrated, maybe even on the edge of burnout. Why? Because you're always trying to do more, and apparently, *it's never quite enough for God.*

Then we hold our church services, begging the Holy Spirit to show up: "Come down into this place. Fall fresh on us. Be with us here, Lord." Subtly, we begin to believe that without carefully crafted music performances and spectacular light shows and significant pleading, God won't arrive on the scene. We carry on in these ways, even though Jesus Himself said that once we found Him, we would never thirst for more of Him again. *Very rarely do we hear about the idea of being satisfied with what we already have in Jesus.*

You're told again and again that you must seek after and achieve closeness to God. You're told to try harder, to get up earlier, to focus your efforts on spiritual disciplines, to do whatever it takes. If you give your all on the effort side, it will surely pay off on the closeness side, right?

All of this is very taxing on your system. You can't handle the frenzy. You can't do the Christian life this way. And you were never meant to! It puts you in a place of *trying* instead of *trusting*.

As a result of this widespread message, we know little about living from God's love and life within us. We end up in crisis mode all the time. We're overwhelmed.

Instead of being energized by the Gospel—which is supposed to be life-giving, liberating, even "easy and light" as Jesus promised—we find ourselves engaged in endless, burdensome efforts to make life work. To all of this, we say: *It doesn't have to be this way.*

THE MESSAGE OF THIS BOOK

This is not a self-help book. It's not about improving yourself. It's not about doing more or being better, getting rid of your bad parts and working on your good ones. No, this book is about discovering who you already are. And it may surprise you.

We're not here to mimic the same "try harder" message you've heard most of your life. We're here with a different message.

Religion says, "You need more." God says, "I've given you everything you need" (2 Peter 1:3). Religion says, "You need to obey God." God says, "Your heart wants to obey Me" (Romans 6:17). Religion says, "You need to love God more." God says, "You have an undying love for Me" (Ephesians 6:24). Religion says, "Try harder to give yourself to God!" God says, "You were bought with a price. You belong to Me in every way. You are My prized possession" (1 Corinthians 6:20; 1 Peter 2:9).

Of course, there are plenty of times we don't feel like these statements from God are true. We experience periods of disillusionment, doubt, and feelings of distance. We ask, "Where is God?"—but we seem to hear nothing but the beating of our own hearts in response.

The hope shared in this book is not a promise that you will always (or even most times) feel great. This book is about trusting the truth of who you really are and letting God convince you that you're much better off than you imagine.

A Behavior-Improvement Program?

You long for something legitimate and liberating, a view of yourself that is both real and radical. In the Gospel, you are given exactly this. God gives you permission to be who you really are. You have the green light to live from your core. You don't have to be what others think you should be. You get to be yourself.

But how can you know who you are when all you've heard about is rule-keeping? You end up thinking the goal of the Christian life is sin prevention and moral living. Perhaps if you just avoid the big sins (pornography, adultery, cheating on your taxes, etc.), you can reach the pinnacle of the faith-based life. You imagine that if you try hard enough, you can arrive at what God really wants from you: reading your Bible, going to church, volunteering for programs, and sharing your faith.

You strive toward this goal, never really knowing what it means to live from the heart. Deep down, you're afraid that who you really are is in conflict with what God wants for you. You adopt a "fake it until you make it" mentality. You believe you don't measure up on the inside, but you figure at least you can look like you do on the outside.

Is Christianity a behavior-improvement program? A sin-management system? A second chance to turn over a new leaf, get your act together, and try to be someone else?

The goal of the Cookie-Cutter Christianity messages we often hear is to press every believer into the same mold. We hope to find comfort in conformity. But here's the problem with that approach: We're suppressing who God made us to be. We're teaching others not to be themselves and to distrust their hearts. We're telling them they need to become more for God, when He's already thrilled with who He's made them to be.

You might think, "Well, I don't feel this new-hearted self you speak of. I'm not sure I have it!" It's perfectly okay if you don't have feelings to confirm what we're saying. Here, we're talking about a knowing, not a feeling. It's truth that sets us free, not emotion. It's the renewing of the mind we're after here, not the experience of certain feelings.

THIS IS FOR YOU

What we propose here is not lofty and distant; this is practical help for anyone and everyone. It's *not* about needing to receive something new. It's not about obtaining a second portion or a second blessing. It's not about getting more of God or a particular spiritual gift. It's as simple as understanding better what God has already done for you and who you already are as a result. And every ounce of what you will discover here is beautifully compatible with normal, everyday life.

What if you don't need to "try harder" or "be changed"? What if the truth is that you have everything you need? You *do* have everything you need (2 Peter 1:3; Ephesians 1:3). The believer's new-hearted self is a plentiful resource and a beautiful instrument. And there is an undeniable liberty in living from your heart.

So there's no need to "get radical" or "get out of your comfort zone" to become someone different or make something new happen.

No, this is for you—right here, right now.

Admittedly, this amazing message is counter to a lot of what we hear today. This is not a message about bettering yourself, nor is it a message about getting rid of yourself. It's not a message about sacrificial living as you push down your own desires. It's not about trying harder or being more. It's not any of those things.

Instead, it's about grasping what God has already accomplished in you. If there is anything to practice, it's the counterintuitive art of "doing nothing"—nothing to get righter, nothing to get cleaner, nothing to get closer, nothing to get "better." The goal is to come to a truth-inspired place of knowing, not merely a place of doing. From this place of believing and knowing, you'll bear fruit, love others, and engage in all that God has for you.

But you'll get there another way.

You have deep spiritual longings etched into the lining of your heart. To unlock them, you don't need "Three Steps to a Better You" or "Five Principles to Fix Your Life." The way forward is both easier and more incredible: You're designed to live from your true desires.

There's room for you in the Christian life. You get to be a part. You get to be the real you, without compromise and without a mask. You're invited.

WHERE WE'RE HEADED

Along the way, you'll need to be vigilant about the thoughts you let into your mind and into your belief system. You'll take on new criteria for what thoughts are acceptable to you in order to rid yourself of the spiritual debris that's so commonplace out there. You'll take up your spiritual sword against the religious-sounding ideas that belittle and accuse your new-hearted self. Consequently, you'll begin to enjoy a freedom and even a lightheartedness about your relationship with God like never before.

How does that sound?

You'll learn to allow the comfort of God's life-giving Spirit to relax you. You'll recognize that His heart is embracing yours, and you'll be astonished to discover the heart-to-heart you already have with Him. Finally, you'll uncover a remarkable capacity to love others as you release your new heart to them. Yes, the perfect you—in union with Jesus—is your greatest asset.

TRANSFORMED LIVES

We're seeing God use this message all over the world to liberate and encourage people. People like you who may be discouraged and hurting—even people who have reached the end of their rope. Maybe you've tried your hardest to find answers, but real peace has eluded you and authentic joy has seemed out of reach.

As we travel and share this message, the response has been beyond what we ever expected. Burnt-out pastors have been revived. Church leaders who felt trapped in a performance-based system have been freed. We've seen lives and marriages restored when things looked grim. Men and women (even teens!) have been liberated to enjoy their relationship with God for the first time. Here are just a few examples from around the world:

> *You've changed my life. I've been a believer for thirty years, and I've finally seen the fruit of the Spirit being produced in my life without effort.* —Doris C. (Texas)

> *Your teachings have simply turned my life around. The revelation of God's boundless love for me has ignited a fresh passion in me for Jesus and made it so easy for me to express truly unconditional love to other people.* —Omoniyi O. (Germany)

> *I shared the message with my husband, and we were both freed from the guilt and the condemnation we had allowed to be put on us. We've since shared with friends, and it's also being relayed to prisoners, and they're being set free!* —Betty B. (Colorado)

> *After many years always focused on sin, I now focus on God's love and I live life, not perfectly, but perfectly content with who I am in Christ.* —Carla L. (Alberta, Canada)

> *Because of you, I know my worth, my value, and the strength I have with Christ in me, seeing it all through the eyes of God.* —Jan F. (Virginia)

I felt that I could never meet God's standards. Every time I failed, I saw myself as disqualified. Then I started looking to your teachings. My sadness started to disappear, little by little. Now, I see things differently, and I'm intrigued to know what I'm going to learn every day. —Karina C. (Venezuela)

If you're looking for real answers that will work, day in and day out, no matter what your circumstances are, this is the book for you. Keep reading. You *won't* be disappointed. This is what you were meant for. This is who you are. This is real hope that you can wholeheartedly embrace. And as you do so, you'll catch glimpses of God smiling with you along the way.

Chapter 2

Several years ago, a single baseball card sold for $3.12 million at Goldin Auctions. Yes, a 1909–1911 Honus Wagner card was valued and sold at that incredible price. The cost to produce the card more than one hundred years ago was less than one cent. And its value continues to rise—at least in the eyes of baseball fans—as the years go by.

To some, the card means nothing. To others, it's nearly priceless. This is a perfect example of how your proposed worth is bestowed upon you by those around you. In the case of the baseball card, collectors esteemed it. In your life, your perceived worth can come from what your father or mother or spouse thinks of you, what your friends or colleagues believe about you, or even what your enemies say about you.

Every one of us has a story of how the labels we took on became our identity, at least for a time. But all these labels have something in common: They're subjective. They come from others. They don't reflect all or even some of what we are. And they say just as much about the person ascribing the value as they do about us. Other people are looking for their own answers in life. They sometimes put labels on us to make themselves feel or look better.

Some of these labels can be positive; others are negative. We compare ourselves with others and end up with no real understanding of our true value.

> *For we are not bold to class or compare ourselves with some of those who commend themselves;* ***but when they measure themselves by themselves and compare themselves with themselves, they are without understanding.*** *(2 Corinthians 10:12)*

You've been propelled by guilt for far too long. You've allowed your past failures to flood your mind and hinder your future. You've taken on labels from those who were never pleased, never satisfied, and never accepted you. They never approved of who you are.

You end up wounded, sometimes even paralyzed by the opinions of those who reject you. Some tell you that transparency and community are the answers to your struggles.

These can help, but they're *not* sufficient.

There are plenty of people who are transparent about their battles and share them with trusted friends. Still, they may continue wallowing in the same rejection and sharing about it. The label they take on is that of a "struggler." Opening up and speaking about their pain is cathartic, but they know little of their new, perfect self and why it matters so much.

It doesn't help that popular flavors of Christianity step in and tell believers: "Deny yourself. God wants to 'break' you. It must be more of Him and less of you." This only adds to the self-loathing we've already engaged in. Now we imagine that God also is labeling us as a failure and rejecting us. All of this ignores the reality of *the perfect you* that we'll discover together in this book. Realizing who we really are is absolutely essential to any genuine healing and fulfillment in this life.

OUR SEARCH

We're all searching for our authentic selves. We want to know:

- Who am I?
- What am I like on the inside?
- What makes me fulfilled?
- What does my future hold?

These questions will never be answered without looking to our Creator. The answers we seek are only found in Him. He is the one who made us. He understands us. And He loves us—exactly as we are.

So instead of chasing someone else's definition of who you are and who you're supposed to be, this book invites you to see yourself from God's vantage point. It's the only view that's completely true. And in turn, what you believe about yourself and your heart will shape everything you do.

We are the creation. To understand ourselves, we must consult the Creator. He's the One who handcrafted us. He knows us intimately. This is why we look to Him to see who we are at the core—not our mirrors, not what other people say about us, not even our self-perception.

God has left nothing to chance. He planned your new life from every angle. In the Gospel, you will discover the profound meaning and purpose of your life. You'll no longer see yourself as an undesirable obstacle to God but as His precious instrument.

Learn Who You Are

You want to live out your destiny. You want to live with confidence and be assured that you're on the right path. But for this to be your experience, you need to know who you really are.

You bring your questions to the world and ask how you stack up. Whether you end up affirmed or shattered, either way, you're asking *the wrong person*.

God designed the Gospel message to affirm and validate you in ways that only He can. Once you cross this threshold of awakening, it changes everything. At first, you may only have information. Over time, you assimilate it into your thinking. Ultimately, it filters into how you envision yourself in a moment of decision.

Anyone who listens to the word but does not do what it says is like someone who looks at his face in a mirror and,

*after looking at himself, goes away and **immediately
forgets what he looks like.*** (James 1:23–24 NIV)

Recognizing this simple truth can be a huge turning point
for you. You don't have to let your wounds from the past
define or label you. Your mind is the battlefield.

It's like having a radio dial within your brain. You can
change the station. You can move from the AM (Alternative Message) stations to the FM (Father's Mentoring)
station. You're offered two distinct signals. Which will you
tune in to?

Here's an important catch: The broadcast of healing truth
from Father's Mentoring channel is being emitted from your
heart. It's what you really want. The other signal comes from
outside of who you are.

AUTHENTIC PERSONHOOD

We're not pushing some sort of positive self-talk that
you might hear from a feel-good preacher on TV: that if
you say it, if you visualize it, if you believe it hard enough,
it will somehow become true for you. No, what we have
to say here is true of every believer whether they realize
it or not.

The Bible says we were originally children of wrath
with depraved minds and wicked hearts. But when you put
your confidence in Jesus and called upon Him to transform
you from the inside out, that's what He did. Exactly what
did God do to you in that moment? We want to share that
with you.

This is about a Christian knowing his authentic person-hood. It's about a believer being inspired the way God designed her to be:

> For you were formerly darkness, but now **you are** Light in the Lord; **walk** as children of Light. (Ephesians 5:8)

As conference speakers, we often hear people say, "You're finally giving words to what I always knew to be true in my heart." Yes, exactly. You already have the Word "planted in you" (James 1:21), but now you get to experience the renewing of your mind to these beautiful truths.

YOUR HEART

We humans often use the term "heart" to refer to the reservoir of passionate or adventurous feelings we might have inside. But here we refer to your spiritual heart, the core of your being where your spiritual longings reside. This is where we are in union with Jesus.

So your spiritual heart is the house of God, much like the Holy of Holies from long ago. Your spiritual heart (or spiritual self) is a pure place. As we'll see, God cleaned house and then moved in.

God went to the "heart" of the matter. He exchanged your spiritual heart in order to transform your whole experience. Now you're simply invited to work out what God has already worked in (Philippians 2:12–13). Genuine growth in attitudes and actions simply means new outward expressions of an already present, inward reality.

The biblical truths in this book will lead you into new motivation for everything you do. You'll learn to live from your innate spiritual instincts even when your feelings don't line up. You'll discover that saying *yes* to your new-hearted self is saying *yes* to the God who gave it to you.

WHAT JESUS PRAYED FOR

The new-hearted self you are today is exactly what Jesus requested of His Father. He prayed you'd have the same closeness that Jesus has with the Father. He asked God for everything you most desire before you even existed. Jesus knew what you needed, and He asked God for it. You didn't play a role in the asking. You're here just for the receiving and enjoying.

> *I do not ask on behalf of these alone, but for those also who believe in Me through their word;* **that they may all be one; even as You, Father, are in Me and I in You, that they also may be in Us,** *so that the world may believe that You sent Me.*
>
> **The glory which You have given Me I have given to them, that they may be one, just as We are one;** *I in them and You in Me, that they may be perfected in unity, so that the world may know that You sent Me, and* **loved them, even as You have loved Me.** *Father, I desire that they also, whom You have given Me,* **be with Me where I am,** *so that they may see My glory which You have given Me, for You loved Me before the foundation of the world.* (John 17:20–24)

We may sometimes doubt whether our own prayers are heard. But we have zero doubt that Jesus got His prayers answered. Here, we see our intimacy with God was Jesus's idea. Yes, the oneness we enjoy with Him was at the heart of our Savior's request. So we don't need to wait to feel something terrific. We can walk in the truth of it today, here and now.

It's not about asking or striving. It's about believing you're clean and close—and counting on it.

CHAPTER 3

Can you say "I am good" without expecting a lightning bolt from Heaven to strike you down? After all, Jesus said no one is good except God (Mark 10:18). But since He said that, our world has experienced His death, His resurrection, and an invitation to a new birth first seen at Pentecost. Do these events not change whether you can now be good?

If only God is good, and you are "born of God" (1 John 5:4), then are you good? If so, to what degree? Is there still a part of you that God rejects? If God rejects sin, does He reject you? Are you partly sinful? Does some part of who you are not make it to Heaven? Can you truly be yourself here and now? These questions have to be answered.

Without hopeful answers, you end up with a message of mediocre news, or maybe something approaching decent

news, but never good news. What we promise in this book is
great news.

Forgiveness of sins is amazing—but it's not enough.
Heaven is amazing—but it's not enough. In the Gospel
message, we see a God who is more than a banker canceling
our debt. He's more than a travel agent changing our itinerary.
He's the Great Physician infusing us with resurrection life.

God didn't merely give you mercy and a new place to go
when you die. As we'll see, He gave you a new desire that
flows from new design. With new desire and new design
comes a whole new way to live.

You can live as the perfect you. And you'll see that Christ
can express Himself perfectly through you even as you're just
being yourself—with no conflict, no disparity, no obstacle.
All the parts of you are a perfect fit together with Him.

This is what the Church's message is missing today. We
know we're *called* to serve. But few of us realize just how
equipped we are to serve. We've been given everything we
need. It's already ours. No asking, no searching, no seeking,
no waiting: It's here and now.

HEART QUESTIONS

You're sitting in church enjoying the worship. The
music leader is at his best, the backup singers are crooning,
the smoke is rolling out, and the music is in full swing.
Then mid-song, the leader pauses for emphasis, looks up
to Heaven, and groans, "God, we've got wicked, wicked
hearts, Lord!"

The congregation erupts with applause and a big "Amen!"

"We're sinners, Lord, desperate for more of You, God!" he continues.

"Yes, Jesus!" everyone responds.

"Purify our hearts today, God, make us clean!" he begs.

"Yes, Lord ..." you start to say along with everyone else.

Then something in the back of your mind makes you stop and wonder: *How many Sundays must I try to get my heart right? How long will I plead for purity? And why are we begging for more of God's presence when He never leaves us?*

You're right to hesitate. Those petitions don't reflect what God actually says about who you are or how to relate to Him.

So is your heart bad or good? Or maybe half good and half bad? Are you part darkness and part light? Perhaps you have two hearts? Two natures, two selves, two sets of desires?

Ask a hundred Christians about the current condition of their heart and answers will vary wildly. Some will shout, "Wicked!" Meanwhile, others claim, "Corrupt and deceitful but under construction!" And here we're saying your heart is *new* and *perfect*.

The state of the believer's heart is central to Christianity itself. After all, Jesus comes to live in our hearts. Isn't that what we believe? So why are our answers all over the place? Why is the subsequent condition of our hearts so unclear? Who's right? How do we know?

WHAT WE HEAR

It's not hard to see why we're confused: We hear the same thing over and over! Visit many churches, pick up many Christian books, or even listen to some worship music, and here's what you'll get: It's all about what you're not doing, and why you should be doing more.

> *You're dirty. You need to get cleaner.*
> *You're distant. You need to get closer.*
> *You're out of fellowship. You need to get back in.*
> *You fell out of God's will for your life. You need to find it.*
> *You need to abide. You need to enter God's rest.*
> *You need the victorious life.*
> *You need. Because you are not okay.*

You're offered lengthy instructions on how to fix yourself. You hear prayers and pleas for God to come closer. You read tips and exhortations on how to think right and act right. In all of this, you receive little—if any—affirmation in the truth that you're already right with God.

"Oh, that's justification. You should already know all of that. We've moved on to sanctification," they might say. So we're supposed to *graduate* from God's grace? And what do we do with passages that say we as believers have already been sanctified?

> *You were sanctified.* (1 Corinthians 6:11)
> *We have been sanctified.* (Hebrews 10:10)

Passages like these get ignored or explained away because they don't fit the narrative of trying to better ourselves.

Meanwhile, we're bombarded with a message of taking new action without taking in new birth. It's a message of change without exchange. It's a feeble gospel of smoke and mirrors, a charade. As we might see in any other world religion, rightness with God supposedly depends on us, our actions, and our choices to improve today. It completely misses the heart of Christianity—the actions God took and the choices He made. In short, it neglects the most important aspect of the Gospel—how God transformed us at the core.

Some of the songs we sing in church only stoke the fires of guilt and shame. Here's one example—a verse from the hymn "Come Thou Fount of Every Blessing," which was written by Robert Robinson in the 1700s. We've sung it hundreds of times over the years:

> *Let that goodness like a fetter*
> *Bind my wandering heart to Thee*
> *Prone to wander, Lord, I feel it*
> *Prone to leave the God I love*
> *Here's my heart, Lord, take and seal it*
> *Seal it for Thy courts above*

Is your heart still prone to wander? Do you still need it to be "taken" and "sealed"? This hymn is based on Psalm 119, in which David is concerned about wandering from the Lord's commandments. But remember that David also pleaded, "Create in me a clean heart" and "do not cast me away from Your Presence" and "do not take your Holy Spirit from me" (Psalm 51).

Why don't Paul or Peter or James or John seem to be concerned about getting their hearts clean or losing God's presence? As a New Testament believer, don't you enjoy something better than what David experienced so long ago?

*And what more shall I say? For time will fail me if I tell of Gideon, Barak, Samson, Jephthah, of **David** and Samuel and the prophets.... And all these, having gained approval through their faith, **did not receive what was promised, because God had provided something better for us,** so that apart from us they would not be made perfect.* (Hebrews 11:32, 39–40)

The cross and the resurrection make a difference. You do enjoy something better today than David ever experienced. As we'll see, it relates to being perfectly forgiven and being made perfect in heart.

What about more modern music? Is it more carefully written to reflect the truth of the Gospel? No—in fact, it actually seems like the problem may be getting worse over time. Overall, most hymns from centuries ago remain truer to the Gospel than a lot of the more contemporary music.

Here's one example from just a few decades ago from the song "Sinner Saved by Grace" by the Gaither Vocal Band:

Now I grow and breathe in freedom
With each breath of life I take
I'm loved and forgiven backed with a living
I'm just a sinner saved by grace
Not worthy to be in God's presence

Are you nothing more than "just a sinner" but "saved by grace"? Are you "loved and forgiven" but "not worthy to be in God's presence"? It's this dirty-worm theology that has kept the truth hidden for far too long.

It's not just our music. This message is pervading Christian culture as a whole. We proudly slap the Christian bumper sticker on our vehicle that says, "I'm not perfect, just forgiven."

We get what this means. We don't perform perfectly. But isn't the whole point of the Gospel that we've been made perfect apart from our performance? Weren't we made perfect by *God's* performance?

CONTRADICTIONS

The result of this "I'm a dirty sinner with a wandering heart" mentality is that we cannot and do not trust our hearts. Furthermore, we're incessantly told we must "examine" and "test" our hearts. Our hearts have many rooms, we're taught, and Jesus is like a spiritual janitor going from room to room, seeking to clean each one up. And who knows what He'll find hiding in the closet!

The takeaway message is: *Watch out for your heart!*

This can leave anyone in a paralysis of analysis, trying to "get right" and "stay right" with God over and over. Many of us no longer experience that confirmation we once felt after "getting right," so we even begin to doubt our salvation.

What we imagine to be the Gospel makes us feel ashamed as it nearly taunts us: "Be good (but you're not good). Try to be like Jesus (even though you're not like Him). Love people more (even though you're unloving and sinful by nature). Ask God to give you a servant's heart (since you don't have one). By the way, you don't pray enough. You don't do enough. And you're not enough."

This creates inner conflict of dramatic proportions. We seek to resolve the contradictory message of "try to be on the outside what you are not on the inside." The end result is guilt and shame. Some of us quit and walk away from formal competition forever. Others of us put a fresh coat of gloss on our masks and plan for yet another day.

Interestingly, in one sense, we're telling believers to become what they're not. On the other hand, we're telling them to get rid of themselves. Yes, some plead with us to kill ourselves spiritually:

Die to self. Deny yourself. Die daily.

So we are the new self, but we should deny our self? Our old self already died with Christ, but we still should die to self? Some of us don't even pause to examine all the contradictions. Of course, there aren't likely any bad intentions among those who teach us wrongly. They're simply offering us the standard fare they were served by those who went before them.

We are relentlessly taught we cannot trust our "self" or our "heart." Our wicked hearts want to stray; therefore, they must be controlled so they can't do what they want. And we have to say *no* to our "self" before we can say *yes* to God.

On the heels of this comes the idea that God's favor on us depends on our choice to purify our hearts. We start to feel that if we do our part first, if we are faithful, then God will do His part. But we must first prove ourselves. The only trouble is that we can never seem to live up to our end of the bargain. We constantly fail. We confess our failures and return to our "duties" only to fail again.

This is not a truthful or edifying message. Rather, it robs us of any spiritual self-worth and power for change in our thinking and choosing. Eventually, we grow disappointed, frustrated, and embittered with the whole thing. After all, if we really are wicked, if our heart truly desires to do what's wrong, there's no hope in sight. We'll be fighting a losing battle our entire lives. So why persevere? If we already have a ticket to Heaven, why not just give up?

Is this the life God intended for us? A fight against ourselves? A constant attempt to clean up what is so very dirty?

No, it's not.

PART 2

THE PERFECT HEART

CHAPTER 4

At salvation, God carried you through a spiritual heart surgery of sorts. As a result, He doesn't need to look at you through special "Jesus glasses." No, He's looking right at you, and He likes what He sees. You're not *merely* "clothed with Christ" like a wolf in sheep's clothing. You're actually a Grade A sheep, through and through.

In short, you're not half and half. You're not good and bad. You're not new and old. You're not righteous and wicked-hearted. Many living out this duality think they are their own worst enemy. You've probably said it yourself. But think about it: If the Bible calls you "a friend of God," then how can you be your own worst enemy?

If your new-hearted self is from God, then what kind of self is it? Would God cause you to be born of Him as someone who is bad, good, or somewhere in the middle?

Jesus said that if even earthly fathers are givers of good gifts, how much more is your heavenly Father a giver of goodness (Luke 11:11–13)? Every good and perfect gift comes from Him (James 1:17). So if God gave you a new-hearted self, then you must be *amazingly* good!

God could've chosen to live anywhere, and He chose you. You're a perfect home for the Spirit of God Himself.

Design Reveals Desire

Once you realize you have a brand-new heart, you start to put the pieces together.

Does your new-hearted self truly desire sin? Does God want you to wrestle it into submission to His wishes through the accountability program you just heard about, or the ten ways to "be radical" and "set yourself apart" offered in that trendy new curriculum, all the while pleading for Him to purify you and return you to His side?

No. All of a sudden, you realize *none* of that makes sense anymore.

You've seen the perfect you.

Remember: If you're recreated in Christ Jesus *for good works* (Ephesians 2:10), then what does that say about your design? You *are* good. And what does this say about your desire? You *want* good. You want what God wants.

Here's what Jesus had to say about how your heart connects to your desire:

> *No **good tree** bears bad fruit, nor does a bad tree bear good fruit. Each tree is recognized by its own fruit.*

*People do not pick figs from thorn bushes, or grapes from briers. **A good man brings good things out of the good stored up in his heart,** and an evil man brings evil things out of the evil stored up in his heart. For the mouth speaks what the heart is full of.* (Luke 6:43–45 NIV)

Jesus Himself says there are indeed "good trees." That's what you are. He goes on to say the "good man" does exist, and there is good in his heart. That's who you are. There is good stored up within you.

Because you're new in Jesus, you have a loving heart. Because you're new in Jesus, you have a kind heart. Because you're new in Jesus, you have a patient heart. You're a loving and kind and patient person by nature. You carry within you all the qualities needed for life and godliness. All of this is true because you're the new-hearted self and bonded to Jesus Christ, who is your life.

> *Seeing that **His divine power has granted to us every-thing pertaining to life and godliness,** through the true knowledge of Him who called us by His own glory and excellence.* (2 Peter 1:3)

> *And **in Him you have been made complete,** and He is the head over all rule and authority.* (Colossians 2:10)

> *When **Christ, who is our life,** is revealed, then **you also will be revealed with Him in glory.*** (Colossians 3:4)

Do You Need More?

We once heard a woman remark that others seem to have "so many spiritual fruits" and she was "lucky to have one." This is a good example of what Christian living has come to mean for so many. We pluralize "fruit of the Spirit" into "fruits" and have in mind a list of traits we should aspire to, one by one, through self-discipline. Then we quantify how we're doing by how many "fruits" we identify in our own conduct.

While there's a beautiful byproduct of having God's Spirit dwell within us, do you see where this goes wrong? Colossians 2:10 says you have been given fullness and you are complete in Christ. If you have everything you need (2 Peter 1:3)—including every spiritual blessing (Ephesians 1:3)—then how many "fruits" are within you? They're all within the perfect you, because Christ Himself lives perfectly within you.

No hunting. No waiting. No begging. We are new-hearted, and we have fullness in Jesus.

Still, we're often exhorted to seek God when we've already found Him. After all, that was Jesus's evangelistic promise: "Seek, and you will find" (Matthew 7:7). We have found Him! We're also told to hunger and thirst for more of God. But Jesus said the opposite: He said if we ate of Him, we would never hunger again. He said if we drank of Him, we would never thirst again (John 6:35). Likewise, we've been told to try to love God more, while Ephesians tells us we already have an *undying* love for God (Ephesians 6:24).

The bottom line is that you don't need anything new, anything different, or anything more. You don't need to look outside yourself for something external to make its way inside you. Instead, you can look within to your new-hearted self where Christ dwells. Right there, you have everything you need (2 Peter 1:3), because you have Him.

With your new heart, you genuinely desire God Himself. Of course, you don't always feel or act that way, but you do always *desire* Him. As a descriptive statement of who you are—*you always love God, and you always love others.* Your new-hearted self never changes.

What this means is nothing short of remarkable. It means you don't need to be pressured, enticed, or manipulated into loving or serving others. As Romans 6:17 says, you have an obedient heart. You have a loving heart. You have a servant's heart. You partake of God's divine nature (2 Peter 1:4; Romans 5:5). A person like that doesn't need to be pushed into loving others.

It's simply who you are.

EASY, NOT HARD

We often feel—or are even told—that living uprightly is an uphill battle because it's striving against ourselves. It's about holding that sacrifice to the flame, because it's always trying to crawl off the altar. We're told to tie ourselves back down to it, and we're constantly reminded that our sacrifices are "not enough."

The popularity of this sort of message is not surprising, given that the world constantly drives us toward "try harder" and "earn" mentalities. But here again, we're called to break with the world's religious perspective. Jesus said His yoke is *easy* and His burden is *light* (Matthew 11:28–30). And here's the secret: Life with God is only "easy and light" when our calling and our design match perfectly. Regardless of what we might hear, that's what God did for us.

Then someone asks: *What would Jesus do?* You follow Him around for a day or two in the four gospels, and you might catch Him tossing furniture, making wine, walking on water, or calling the Pharisees "snakes." But displaying the new-hearted self is not about imitating the actions of Jesus two thousand years ago. It's less about asking "What would Jesus do?" than it is about asking "What is Jesus doing right now as He's one spirit with me?" So you don't have to "try to be like Jesus." In a very real sense, you *have* become like Him (1 John 4:17). Now you're called to learn who you are in Him and then simply be yourself.

DESIRE, NOT DISCIPLINES

Living from your new-hearted, perfect self means you don't need to *try* to know God. In a spiritually intuitive way, you *do* know Him:

> *As for you, the anointing which you received from Him abides in you,* **and you have no need for anyone to teach you; but as His anointing teaches you about all things,** *and is true and is not a lie, and just as it has taught you, you abide in Him.* (1 John 2:27)

> *No longer will they teach their neighbor, or say to one another, 'Know the Lord,' because* **they will all know**

me, *from the least of them to the greatest.* (Hebrews 8:11 NIV)

Furthermore, learning and communicating with God are not "disciplines." They're the true longings of your heart. Now, don't get us wrong. We know there are sermon series and books aplenty extolling the virtues of the so-called "spiritual disciplines" from Bible study to prayer to service. But here's the thing: Why do we call them "disciplines" when the Bible itself does not? That's right; while there's a place for bodily discipline and God's discipline, learning about God and talking to Him are never referred to as "disciplines" in the New Testament.

Then there's the question of what the word "disciplines" implies: that we don't really want to do them. So through "disciplines" we force ourselves to pursue—*against our desire*—what God wants us to do. In reality, nothing could be further from the truth.

Imagine that, as a child, your parents go on a long trip, leaving you behind. After the first two weeks, you start to really miss them! Then your phone rings. It's them calling from overseas. You answer the phone and say, "Dad, I don't really want to talk to you, but everyone around me says I should 'discipline myself' to talk to you more, so I answered the phone."

Then you get a fat letter from them, postmarked with foreign stamps. You think, "I really should open the letter … but I don't feel like it. Maybe if I follow this three-step accountability plan, I'll be able to open the letter in a few days.

And if I discipline myself regularly, maybe I could bring myself to read as much as five lines a day."

Absurd, right? They're your parents! You love them. You miss them. You can't wait to talk to them, to tell them everything that's been happening with you and hear what they've been doing. Of course you want to hear from them and talk to them. So when that letter arrives, you rip it open and devour it in one sitting. Maybe you even go back to it a few times so you can feel as if they're right there with you.

When it's our earthly family, we call it "talking to them." But when it's our heavenly Father, we have unique and intimidating words—"prayer" and "spiritual disciplines"—that can cloud our perspective. Isn't prayer just talking to our Dad? What is Bible study, other than reading His love letter to us?

So, if you're inundated with pressure, guilt, and even manipulation at times, you may never realize your true desire to pray (talk to your Dad) and read the Bible (His letter to you). If you're constantly told it is your "Christian duty," it inevitably becomes *less* desirable, not more. Everything you do, from living to giving, can and should be done freely, without any pressure:

> *Each one must do just as he has purposed in his heart,* **not grudgingly or under compulsion,** *for God loves a cheerful giver.* (2 Corinthians 9:7)

What if we could see that learning from God's Word is like eating great food and that prayer is like talking to your most trusted best friend? It's all about the perspective, isn't it?

God invites you to be freely inspired from your new-hearted, perfect self in an atmosphere of genuine freedom.

CHAPTER 5

"I've got it all up here in my head. I just need to get it down here in my heart."

People we meet say this all the time. Somehow we've gotten the impression that we have it all upstairs (in our heads) and that what we lack is having it all in our heart.

But that's actually *backwards*!

We don't have it all upstairs. We're still experiencing the renewing of our minds. That's a process that's in progress. We're learning and growing in the knowledge of Jesus. But we actually *do* have it all deep down in our hearts.

You've undergone a heart transplant, a DNA swap at the root of your being. That surgery is over; it's finished. It's the renewing of your thought life that is in process. So next time someone says, "I've got it all up here," run for the hills! No one has it all in their head. If they did, they'd be a know-it-all.

Yes—you do have it all, but not up in your head. Just look one foot below to your spiritual heart. That's where all wisdom and spiritual blessings reside in the person of Jesus. And those beautiful truths have already begun to percolate up to your head.

So while your prayer can be, "Father, renew my mind," at the same time you can also pray, "Teach me what it means to possess all of You all the time in my new-hearted, perfect self."

HEART ATTACK

It seems there's an attack on believers' hearts these days. The enemy appears to have convinced many Christians that our hearts are "deceitfully wicked." We even think we're being humble to see ourselves that way. But real humility is saying the same thing about yourself that God says—no more *and no less.*

If you truly want to understand your heart, you need to inquire of the God of the universe. Is your heart still sinful, dirty, and wrong? Or, through new birth, has your heart been made new and blameless and good? If it is new, then what implications might this have for you as you begin making this one-foot journey from head to heart and start living from the perfect you?

As we process this fundamental yet revolutionary idea that you are now good—through and through—here are more questions we'll explore. First, can you trust your heart? Is there really a go-to place within you that you can count on? Or is that just wishful thinking? Second, do you really have all the resources you need for life and godliness within you?

Or do you need to resign yourself to more of those "long-distance phone calls" in which you ask God to swoop down out of Heaven to visit you with a new portion of love or patience for the day?

Let's start with a heart exam.

YOUR HEART EXAM

Can you trust your heart? The answer to this question isn't found in your past experiences, your most recent performance, or your current emotions. You may *feel* as if you can't trust your heart. Things you've done in the past may suggest you shouldn't. Even the choices you made yesterday may make you shout to yourself, "Don't trust your heart!"

But we're not asked to look to our track records. Instead, the author of Hebrews tells us that if we want to know the thoughts and intentions of our hearts, there's one place to look: the Word of God.

> *The word of God is living and active and sharper than any two-edged sword and **the word of God is able to judge the thoughts and the intentions of the heart.*** (Hebrews 4:12)

If you truly want to know what kind of heart you have, only the Word of God can give you an accurate answer. Through this book, we're asking God to reveal to you the nature and the composition of your spiritual heart.

Imagine if we were to open you up on a spiritual operating table. What would you look like on the inside? What would

we see inside you? As we ask these questions together, you'll
learn some incredible truths that may surprise you.

Do You Want to Sin?

There's a place within you where Christ lives. It's a pure
place much like the holy of holies from the Old Testament.
This is how your body has become the temple of the Holy
Spirit.

God cleaned house, and then He moved in:

> *"For this is the covenant that I will make with the house*
> *of Israel after those days," says the Lord:*
> *"I will put My laws into their minds,*
> *And I will write them on their hearts.*
> *And I will be their God,*
> *And they shall be My people."* (Hebrews 8:10)

God decided to write His desires on your heart so you
would truly want what He wants. If you don't fully understand what we're saying yet, we want to offer you one thought
to really drive this home. We ask you to consider the following
statement. It's short, but nevertheless we invite you to wrestle
with the implications of it. Here it is for you to say aloud:

I don't really want to sin.

Yes, that's right: We're saying that you don't really want
to sin. And you never will. This may be difficult to say. It may
feel impossible to believe. But let's play out this possibility, as
well as the popular alternative.

If your heart truly, deeply, and irrevocably desires to sin—anywhere, anytime—then frankly, there's no hope for you on this side of Heaven. It is impossible for you to live contrary to your desires and contrary to your true self for your remaining years. For now, why not just "eat, drink, and be merry" until you die? You can't consistently go against your own self anyway: A house divided against itself cannot stand (Matthew 12:25).

However, if you've undergone a heart transplant, then your desires have likewise been exchanged. If the core of your spiritual being has been ripped out and replaced, then so have your spiritual passions. And this is why you will *never* be satisfied by sin.

Have you noticed? First, during temptation, there is a stirring within you, a war. Something is not quite right. There's an argument taking place. You're not 100 percent ready to move forward with the idea. You feel like you're fighting against something.

Then, after you give in to the temptation, are you at peace, pleased with what you've done? Or do you instead find yourself asking, "Why did I do that?" This says a great deal about your true wants and desires. Still, you end up sinning. You're deceived, and in the process, you end up acting contrary to the new-hearted, perfect you.

*You don't really **want** to sin. Your heart is not in it.*

Unfortunately, that's a newsflash in the Christian world today. Most Christian teaching starts with the premise that you want to sin, but you shouldn't. You want to sin, but you're not supposed to. Ultimately, this can lead you to a fake-it-until-you-make-it theology: *You're essentially sinful,*

but you better not sin. Your heart is wicked, but don't you do
anything wicked!

But God is not asking you to fake anything. Every ounce
of the instruction we see in the New Testament is a perfect
description of who you already are on the inside. With each
instruction, God is simply saying, "Here's the way to express
the deep, heartfelt desires I implanted within you. This will
fulfill you and meet the needs of those around you."

New Possibilities!

A new-hearted self means new possibilities. You really can
live from your core passions and desires. Here again is one
example of where you're invited to do so!

> *Each one must do **just as he has purposed in his heart**,*
> *not grudgingly or under compulsion, for God loves a*
> *cheerful giver.* (2 Corinthians 9:7)

What does this say about your heart? It suggests that the
purposes of your heart are good and fully aligned with God's
will. Say that one aloud: *The purposes of my heart are aligned*
with God's will.

Paul also says the goal of his instruction is love from a pure
heart (1 Timothy 1:5). How could that even begin to happen
unless your heart is new and pure? Likewise, Peter writes,
"but let it be the hidden person of the heart, with the imperishable quality of a gentle and quiet spirit, which is precious
in the sight of God" (1 Peter 3:4). How could you afford to let

it be "the hidden person of the heart" if your heart were bad? You couldn't.

In passages like these, God is essentially offering you a spiritual X-ray machine. He's showing you who you are on the inside. Imagine if you prayed, "God, reveal to me the hidden person of my heart. Show me who I am." These verses are His answer!

Romans 5 says the love of God has been poured into your heart. Is the love of God residing in a wicked heart? Ephesians 3 says that Christ dwells in your heart through faith. Does Christ dwell in a dirty place? Galatians 4 says God has sent forth the Spirit of His Son into your heart. Did God send the Spirit of Christ to live in a filthy-hearted sinner?

No. The unbeliever may lay awake at night dreaming of new ways to sin. They seem totally fine with it. But here you are, doing whatever you can to find solid answers to avoid sin. You're different. You're an alien and a stranger in this world (1 Peter 2:11). And God wants you to know it. His Spirit is bearing witness with your spirit that you are part of the Family now, and you're a perfect fit (Romans 8:16).

You can rightly say, "I belong to You, Father. You've won my heart. Now it belongs to You. I'm in Your family. I'm invited to Your table. Your Spirit within me reveals my true identity."

Remember—salvation is not just forgiveness and Heaven. Salvation means that you are different at the root of your being. God has done something radical to you. And you will spend a lifetime and more probing the depths of all that it means for you.

God longs to convince you. He wants you to know the deeper truths of the Gospel. He will stop at nothing to reveal them to you. He's firmly committed to your experiencing your newness and union with Him. It is His heart's cry (and yours!) that you taste the essence of who you are in Him and all the beauty that is spiritually simmering below the surface. God wants you to embrace and enjoy your new-hearted self—the perfect you.

CHAPTER 6

What did our spiritual hearts look like before salvation? We once had an unregenerate heart that desired evil. We were slaves to sin—addicted to it. Romans 1 says, "God gave them over in *the lusts of their hearts*" (Romans 1:24). Apparently, our hearts lusted after sin, longed for it, craved it.

You might think, "Yes, that's me. I can't stop thinking about sin. I want to sin." But we encourage you to rethink that one.

Here in Romans 1, Paul is 100 percent clear that this is a description of the *unbeliever*, not the believer. Are you born again with a lustful heart? Did God gift you with a new yet sinful heart? Do you have two spiritual hearts?

No. Don't take this scripture to heart in that way. Remember that you're essentially reading someone else's mail. You're reading a description of someone else who is *not you*.

Does your heart crave sin 24/7? Are you never satisfied unless you're sinning? After you're done, are you happy you did it and cannot wait to do it again? If you're a new creation in Christ, it's impossible for you to consistently believe that (1 John 3:9). You may think you want to sin, but when you do, you are dissatisfied. It never *really* fulfills you.

Elsewhere, Paul again speaks of an unbeliever's heart: "being darkened in their understanding, excluded from the life of God because of the ignorance that is in them, because of *the hardness of their heart*" (Ephesians 4:18). Again, it is the *unbeliever* who is disconnected from the life of God.

Their heart is hard.

But how often have you heard Christians—even pastors— telling another believer that their heart is hard? Not true! Sure, we sometimes harbor hardened attitudes of bitterness or resentment in the mind, but we believers have *new* and *obedient* and *soft* hearts (Ezekiel 36:26; Romans 6:17).

Romans 2 says, "But because of your stubbornness and *unrepentant heart* you are storing up wrath for yourself in the day of wrath and revelation of the righteous judgment of God" (verse 5). Here, the unbeliever's heart is described as *unrepentant.*

But in opening your heart to Jesus Christ, you expressed repentance from the old and dead way of living. You turned toward faith in God and began a new life with Jesus. So you as a believer are not unrepentant by nature. Think about it: You can't have an obedient heart and an unrepentant heart at the same time.

Furthermore, we know from Romans 5 that we believers are *saved from wrath.* Therefore, Romans 2 is clearly not about those who are God's children. It is only the unbeliever who is unrepentant at heart and experiences wrath.

YOUR NEW, OBEDIENT HEART

God's way starts with inward change, not outward behavior modification. Physical circumcision was a Jewish surgery, a cutting away. New life in Christ involves a surgery on your spiritual heart. It is a cutting away of your old heart and a giving of your new heart by God's Spirit.

> But he is a Jew who is one inwardly; and **circumcision is that which is of the heart, by the Spirit**, not by the letter; and his praise is not from men, but from God. (Romans 2:29)

Later in the same letter, Paul says this about your heart:

> But thanks be to God that though you were slaves of sin, you became **obedient from the heart** to that form of teaching to which you were committed, and having been freed from sin, you became **slaves of righteousness**. (Romans 6:17–18)

When you hear that you've got a wicked heart, you can respond with, "No, I've got an obedient heart. I'm a slave of righteousness!"

Yes, you used to be a slave of sin. And that slavery was so very real—your heart craved sin. You had passion in your heart for sin. That's who you *were*. But this new slavery is just as real. Your heart craves dependency on Jesus. You have a passion for Him. This is who you are now.

Here's another way to say it: "nor thieves, nor the covetous, nor drunkards, nor revilers, nor swindlers will inherit the kingdom of God. Such *were* some of you; but you were *washed*, but you were *sanctified*, but you were *justified* in the name of the Lord Jesus Christ and in the Spirit of our God" (1 Corinthians 6:10–11).

You *were* those things by nature. You *were* those things at heart. But now everything has changed for you. You're not the same person anymore.

THE HEART SURGERY OF SALVATION

In Ezekiel 36, we find an ancient prophecy speaking of a heart transplant:

> *Moreover, I will give you a new heart and put a new spirit within you; and I will **remove the heart of stone from your flesh and give you a heart of flesh**.* (Ezekiel 36:26)

Notice a few incredible things here. First and foremost, at salvation, you undergo a heart surgery. You get *a new heart.* That's right—the heart that was lustful, hard, and unrepentant before salvation is *gone.* You don't have that heart anymore.

The "wicked heart" is certainly discussed in the Bible— but the Bible is also clear that *you don't have it anymore.* It was surgically removed and replaced with a brand-new heart. That's what salvation accomplished.

But that's not all. Ezekiel 36 has something else in it, something amazing. It says that you get *a new spirit* too. Did you notice the word "spirit" is not capitalized? This word "spirit" is lowercase here, because it does *not* refer to the Holy Spirit. It refers to *your human spirit*.

What is your human spirit? It's your spiritual core, the place where your spiritual heart resides with its passions and desires. More on this later! But for now, this means there was a complete transformation of who you are at the center of your being. You had an old human spirit that was *dead to God and alive to sin*. Now you have a new human spirit that is *dead to sin and alive to God*. In addition, you have the Holy Spirit living in you.

Many have streamed down the aisle in church to "be saved," believing they received nothing more than forgiveness of sins and a new place to go when they die. Perhaps some realize they received the Holy Spirit too, but even then, they may imagine something like a dollop of Holy Spirit whipped cream on top of their current self (perhaps to look better in God's eyes). But that's not what this prophecy in Ezekiel portrays. Far from it!

At salvation, the core of your being was ripped out and replaced. You used to be a sinner by nature. Now you're a saint. You have become the righteousness of God (2 Corinthians 5:21). As we'll see in detail, this metamorphosis happened, because it wasn't just Christ who died on that cross. Spiritually, *you* somehow died with Him.

This Page in the Book

Consider the page you're reading right now—the page in this book. If you were to throw this book into a fire and burn it up, what would happen to this page? It too would be burned. Why? Because the page is in the book. If you were to dig a hole and bury this book, what would happen to this page? It too would be buried because the page is in the book. If you were to raise this book up and seat it on a very high shelf, what would happen to this page? It too would be raised and seated on the shelf. Why? Again, because the page is in the book.

Likewise, you are in Christ. As a result of being in Christ, you were crucified, buried, and raised in Him. What happened to Him happened to you spiritually.

> ***Or do you not know that all of us who have been baptized into Christ Jesus have been baptized into His death?*** *Therefore we have been buried with Him through baptism into death, so that as Christ was raised from the dead through the glory of the Father,* ***so we too might walk in newness of life.*** *For if we have become united with Him in the likeness of His death, certainly we shall also be in the likeness of His resurrection, knowing this, that* ***our old self was crucified with Him,*** *in order that our body of sin might be done away with, so that we would no longer be slaves to sin;* ***for he who has died is freed from sin.*** *(Romans 6:3–7)*

"Or do you not know ... ?" That's how this passage begins. Apparently, something can be true of you, but you

don't know about it. That's exactly what we're saying throughout this book—something dramatic has happened to you, and
you may not even realize it.

The baptism here in Romans 6 has nothing to do with
water. It's about being spiritually immersed in Christ. Just as
the page was "baptized" into this book, you have been baptized into Jesus Christ. It's this placement into Christ that
made it possible for you to undergo a radical surgery at the
root of your being.

Salvation doesn't merely involve Jesus dying for your sins.
Salvation includes *you dying with Jesus*. Galatians 2:20 says, "I
have been crucified with Christ." Romans 6:6 says, "Our old
self was crucified with Him." Colossians 2:20 says, "You died
with Christ."

This message—that the old self died, that we have been
crucified with Christ—was so essential, so central to the
Gospel message that Paul made sure to write about it and
repeat it, again and again, in his letters.

The old you no longer lives. The new you now lives by
faith in Jesus. The old you was taken to the cross, crucified,
and buried. The new you longs to live in dependence on Him.

Salvation is nothing less than you dying and waking up
with a new-hearted self: the perfect you bonded to Jesus forever. Forgiveness was not enough. You had to die and rise
again with Christ.

This is *the other half of the Gospel*.

"Jesus died and rose again for you" is just part of the Gospel, the part we all hear in church. But "you died and rose
again with Jesus" is the other part, the part we rarely hear.

Yet it's the secret to knowing the perfect you.

Don't Reject Yourself

If we're not discerning in what we believe, we end up taking on doctrines that cause us ultimately to reject ourselves. The word "self" becomes a dirty word for us. We strive to put down "self" and eventually kill "self" in our pursuit of God, not realizing God has already done away with and replaced that old self. He simply wants us to believe it and act on it: "Even so consider yourselves to be dead to sin, but alive to God in Christ Jesus" (Romans 6:11).

What's the end result of that morbid message? We end up believing we're unacceptable in God's sight and that the only reason He tolerates us for even a second is because He's looking at us through a Jesus filter. If He were to take away the filter for even a moment, He would see us for who we truly are: detestable sinners, saved by grace but always desiring to return to our former evil ways. We conclude that we have to keep a tight grip on our hearts because they constantly desire to lead us in the wrong direction.

All the while, the Gospel truth is this: You've *truly* been born again (1 Peter 1:3). You are born of the Spirit (John 3:6). You are a child of the resurrection (Luke 20:36). You are a slave of righteousness (Romans 6:17). You are a partaker of the divine nature (2 Peter 1:4). You are one spirit with Jesus (1 Corinthians 6:17). You have been given a new heart and a new spirit and God's Spirit (Ezekiel 36:26–27). That's the Gospel truth about who you really are!

Sure, Jesus paid the price, but that price was not the cost of designing a specialized filter for God to look through. It was the cost of *fundamentally transforming who you are at your very root.* It was the cost of making you genuinely forgiven, genuinely righteous, and genuinely—not "positionally" but completely and truly—good.

PART 3

THE PERFECT SELF

CHAPTER 7

The documentary film *Waste Land* (2010) details the lives of men and women who live in the largest landfill in the world, a trash dump just outside Rio de Janeiro. Every day they wake up and sift through the garbage to find something—anything—to eat and survive. Some of them have even made makeshift dwellings from the trash. If they had a choice, would they live there? Of course not! No one wants to live in a dump. This seems obvious, right?

God doesn't choose to live in dirty places either. You're not a dump. You're His holy and righteous and blameless vessel, through and through (Ephesians 5:27). You're not trash. You're His temple (1 Corinthians 6:19).

Think about it: No passage of Scripture even remotely insinuates that you get a last-minute heart transplant right before you enter Heaven. There's no exchange of heart, exchange of spirit, or exchange of soul at the Pearly Gates. What does this mean? It can only mean that everything that needed to happen to you—apart from a new body, of course— has *already* happened.

You are new right now (2 Corinthians 5:17). You're united with Christ (Romans 6:5). And you are fully *compatible* with Him.

Aren't We Still "Sinners"?

So many sermons, hymns, and Christian books refer to us as "sinners." To say this about ourselves sounds self-deprecating and maybe even super-spiritual or godly to some. But it's simply not consistent with God's truth.

The Gospel announces that you as a believer are not a sinner by nature anymore. You are a saint who sometimes sins. And yes, there's a big difference. But the question remains: Will you believe what God says about you is actually real and true? Or will you just imagine it to be some pretend, "feel good" view of you? Or perhaps it's just a heavenly condition you'll have one day, but it hasn't been activated yet?

When we speak at conferences, we often ask people: "Is there anyone here who never sins?" If anyone raises their hand, we respond with, "Well, now you have!" Of course, we all commit sins. If we say we don't, we're lying—and that's a sin! But as children of God, we are not what we *do*. Let that play through your mind:

I am NOT the sum total of what I do.

This can be difficult to grasp because so many identities you see in this world *are* built on what people do. You have a child, and that makes you a parent. You work as a teacher or a salesperson or a small business owner, and you think that makes you who you are. When you commit a crime, you're called a criminal. When you're addicted to alcohol, you're called an alcoholic.

But God does *not* define you by your behavior. You might struggle with something, but He doesn't define you as a "struggler." You are His child. And even though you commit sins, He doesn't call you a sinner. He calls you a saint. And He's not faking Himself out either!

CHIEF OF SINNERS?

But doesn't the Apostle Paul call himself the "chief of sinners"? If all that we've been saying is true, then how could Paul call himself a sinner instead of a saint?

> *I thank Christ Jesus our Lord, who has strengthened me, because He considered me faithful, putting me into service, **even though I was formerly a blasphemer and a persecutor and a violent aggressor.** Yet I was shown mercy because I acted ignorantly in unbelief; and the grace of our Lord was more than abundant, with the faith and love which are found in Christ Jesus. It is a trustworthy statement, deserving full acceptance, that **Christ Jesus came into the world to save sinners, among whom I am foremost of all. Yet for this reason I found mercy,** so that in me as the foremost, Jesus Christ might demonstrate His perfect patience as an example for those who would believe in Him for eternal life. (1 Timothy 1:12–16)*

Paul is referring to his *former* life as a blasphemer, persecutor, and violent aggressor. These things were true of him *before* salvation. But while Paul was the foremost (chief) of sinners, he found mercy, and the result was eternal life. In other words, he was transformed into a saint. So Paul would never call himself the "chief of sinners" as a believer. Remember that Paul never calls believers "sinners" in *any* of his letters. He always refers to us as saints.

Someone may point out the present-tense verb in "I *am* the foremost of all." Doesn't this mean Paul was speaking of his current state as an apostle?

Imagine Michael Jordan being interviewed at age eighty-five. He might say, "I am the best NBA basketball player of all time." But Michael Jordan is no longer an NBA player. So why would he phrase it that way? He would simply be saying that he set enough records in his mind to qualify as the best NBA player in history. He doesn't need to be a current player to state that.

Likewise, the Apostle Paul was saying that he set a record as an unbeliever as the foremost of sinners. But at the time of writing his epistle, even though he still held the record, he would no longer refer to himself as a sinner. He was now a saint who sometimes sinned. He was formerly a blasphemer and violent aggressor, but now he was reborn as a new-hearted child of God.

And you are too!

You're a Saint!

Your surname comes from your physical birth or your adopted parents, indicating you are part of the family no matter what you do. In the same way, your identity as a child of God comes from your new birth and your adoption into His family. No matter what you might do, you're part of the family now.

The word "sinner" appears more than a dozen times in the New Testament epistles, but it never refers to a believer. You aren't a sinner anymore. You're dead to that family now. Instead, you're a member of God's family. Although you sometimes sin, you're a saint.

Let's face it. If you were defined and labeled by your past performance, there wouldn't be much motivation to keep going. You'd be such a dirty failure that you'd eventually just commit more sins because you'd think: *Why not? I'm already so messed up, why not throw one more sin on the pile?*

But because you are righteous by birth, you wake up every day perfectly right (righteous) with God and perfectly forgiven and cleansed. Each day is a new opportunity to make better choices and live free from sin's grip. As we'll see, it's incredibly motivating not only to be "seen" this way by God, but for it to *actually be true of you* at the core.

So if you're a *believer*, you don't have to push down your desires. Instead, you can acknowledge them and live from them.

You can be yourself and express Jesus at the same time!

A FRAGRANT AROMA

Still, many believers carry on seeing themselves as dirty vessels. Maybe God has to pinch His nose in order to live with their stench! But there's really nothing odorous about us as believers. Apparently, God actually likes how we smell:

For we are a fragrance of Christ to God among those
who are being saved and among those who are perishing.
(2 Corinthians 2:15)

When you call yourself "a dirty sinner," you're not giving
God the credit He deserves for what He has done to you. For
you, "self" is not a dirty word. It's a beautiful word. You're the
new self—and only one self—and you're compatible with the
God of the Universe.

You are a unique person that God made—a person who
is different from everyone else on the planet, but a person who
is perfectly in tune with God's desires and heart: The *perfect*
you is a *perfect* fit for a *perfect* relationship with Him!

So you don't need to be afraid of yourself. You also don't
need to be afraid of your "own resources" or abilities or talents.
(Some carry a morbid view of abilities and talents, as they
chalk them up to being opposed to God at work in our lives!)
Remember that you are not an obstacle; you are an instrument. And as we'll see, you don't need to get rid of yourself
or push yourself down.

Maybe you've been asked: "What would you change about
yourself?" Well, do you know what God's answer concerning
you would be? "Nothing." He would change nothing about
you. Because He already transformed you, you're already
exactly who He wants you to be. He made sure of it!

A One-Foot Journey to the Perfect You

So God invites you on a one-foot journey. It's a journey
from head to heart. Right now, you may tend to live from your

"headspace" and all the thoughts currently in there. The current version of your thinking can run your life.

You let it run the way you do marriage. You let it run the way you do relationships. You let it run the way you do your listening and your communication. But God calls you to live from another place, not merely from your head but from your heart.

However, this one-foot journey becomes difficult if you believe your heart is untrustworthy. This journey from head to heart becomes nearly impossible if you believe your heart is dirty and sinful and even distant from God.

You need to inquire of the God of the universe concerning the nature of your new-hearted self.

Is your heart still sinful, dirty, wicked, and wrong? Or, through new birth, has your heart been made new and right and blameless? And if so, what implications does this have for you as you take this one-foot journey from head to heart and begin living from your core?

- The one-foot journey to a better life
- The one-foot journey to better communication
- The one-foot journey to better relationships

Sometimes, we seek to relate to others via our "headspace" alone. We only employ our gray matter. In arguing, we try to prosecute and win. We bicker. We compete with each other. We use our current coping mechanisms.

We operate in this headspace and prosecute the other person with evidence of why we're right and they're wrong. Then they take up the role of defending themselves and prosecuting us. We each state our case, defend our position, and present the evidence.

We seek to win ... and then *everybody* loses.

We seek to win, and the marriage loses. We seek to win, and the church loses. We seek to win, and the friendship loses. Why? Because we're operating from our current mental understanding of how to cope and make life work instead of living from the heart.

Your heart is a safe place for you. It is where Christ lives. God cleaned house. Then He moved in. He is trustworthy. And as the new self, so are you!

CHAPTER 8

Over the years, theologians have debated whether the believer's righteousness is merely *imputed* (counted toward us) or if it is *imparted* (actually given to us).

Imputed righteousness means that your standing with God is like a matter of accounting. God has credited righteousness to your heavenly bank account while you're here on Earth awaiting a future inner transaction.

Imparted righteousness is the idea that God has already transformed you in some way, causing you to actually be righteous by nature.

IT'S A BOTH-AND!

The simple truth is that both of these ideas appear in some form in the Bible. First, Romans tells us that righteousness was imputed (credited) to Abraham and to anyone who believes:

> For what does the Scripture say? "Abraham believed God, and it was **credited** to him as righteousness." Now to the one who works, his wage is not credited as a favor, but as what is due. But to the one who does not work, but believes in Him who justifies the ungodly, his faith is **credited** as righteousness, just as David also speaks of the blessing on the man to whom God **credits** righteousness apart from works. (Romans 4:3–6)

This kind of righteousness alone is enough to excite anyone. Righteousness credited to you apart from good works you might do? Wow! That's incredible! Still, there's more to get excited about. Galatians says that righteousness was not merely credited to you but actually *imparted* (given) to you at salvation:

> Is the Law then contrary to the promises of God? May it never be! For if a law had been given which was able to **impart life, then righteousness** would indeed have been based on law. But the Scripture has shut up everyone under sin, so that the promise by faith in Jesus Christ might be given to those who believe. (Galatians 3:21–22)

Notice that "life" and "righteousness" are near synonyms in this passage. The Old Testament law was not able to impart life to you. Instead, you received life by faith in Jesus Christ. Now did you catch how you became righteous? You became righteous *when life was imparted to you.* This means you don't merely have a "bank account" type of righteousness. You have an "imparted life" type of righteousness too.

A SLAVE BY BIRTH

Think about it: If you're truly "born again" (John 3:3) and "born of God" (John 1:12–13) and "born of the Spirit" (John 3:6), doesn't that mean a real transformation occurred inside you? If God Himself gave birth to you spiritually, wouldn't that make you *actually* righteous?

Yes. You were unrighteous by birth (in Adam). You're now righteous by new birth (in Christ). You have a birth-based righteousness. This is why the Apostle John speaks this way about you:

> *Little children, make sure no one deceives you; the one who practices righteousness **is righteous, just as He is righteous**.* (1 John 3:7)

How righteous is Jesus? What type of righteousness does He have? Is it merely imputed (credited) righteousness? Or is righteousness actually part of His nature? Because Jesus is the Son of God, we easily agree that He is actually righteous. Now do you see that John equates your righteousness with that of Jesus? There's something profound for you to see here!

But can we really be sure? Paul helps us gain even more certainty:

> *But thanks be to God that though **you were slaves of sin**, you became obedient from the heart to that form of*

teaching to which you were committed, and having been
*freed from sin, **you became slaves of righteousness.***
(Romans 6:17–18)

How real was your slavery to *sin*? Very real. So how real
is your slavery to *righteousness*? Just as real! Think about everything that came with being a slave of sin. It wasn't just a
tendency to sin. It was an intrinsic *connection* to sin. We
couldn't help it. We were *controlled* by sin. Sin consumed us.
Likewise, we now have an intrinsic connection to righteousness. We can't help it. We are controlled by righteousness.
Righteousness consumes us.

REALLY RIGHTEOUS

Here's a similar passage where Paul compares our life in
Adam to our life in Jesus:

For as through the one man's disobedience the many were
***made sinners,** even so through the obedience of the One*
*the many will be **made righteous.*** (Romans 5:19)

It was Adam's disobedience that made you a sinner by
nature. Likewise, it was Christ's obedience on the cross and
through the resurrection that made you righteous by nature.

Did the disobedience of Adam simply "credit" sinfulness
to your spiritual bank account? Or were you *literally* and *actually* a sinner because of Adam? Of course, you literally and
actually became a sinner through Adam. Sin was passed down
through the ages to you from him. You were born in Adam

and therefore born in sin. This reality impacted you in every spiritual way, permeating your spiritual self and desires. You wanted to sin. And you couldn't escape the slavery of it. You were a sinner, not just positionally but actually.

Similarly, through Christ, you were reborn and thereby made righteous. The Greek word for "made" in "made righteous" in Romans 5:19 means "to appoint" or "to cause to be." God appointed you as His child—not because He started pretending you were righteous, but because through new birth He caused you to really *be* righteous.

You want to display righteousness, and you can't escape the slavery of it. You're permanently bonded to Jesus at the very root of your new-hearted self. You're actually a saint.

OR DO YOU NOT KNOW?

"Yeah, but I just don't feel like a slave of righteousness." Fair enough. We don't feel it either, but it's not a feeling. It's a fact.

Imagine if you were to interview ten unbelieving friends and ask them if they feel like slaves of sin. What types of responses do you imagine you might receive? One response might be, "Slave of sin? No, I can't relate to that in the slightest. I very much feel like a free agent on this planet, and I can do all kinds of good." Another might say, "I do more good than bad, for sure. I'm a pretty good person really. So no, I don't feel controlled by some sinister force called sin."

Even with responses like these, wouldn't you still think that unbelievers are "slaves of sin"? Yes, despite their lack of awareness, you would hold to the biblical teaching and believe the truth. So might it be possible that you are a slave of righteousness, but you're just not aware of it on an emotional (or mental) level? Maybe this is what the Apostle Paul had in mind when he asked in Romans 6:1–3:

> *What shall we say then? Are we to continue in sin so that grace may increase? May it never be!* **How shall we who died to sin still live in it?** *Or do you not know that all of us who have been baptized into Christ Jesus have been baptized into His death?*

The Roman believers were questioning what motivation they had for godly living if God's grace was unconditional and inexhaustible. With unconditional love, total forgiveness of sins, and eternal life promised no matter what, why not just go out and set world records for sin? That's the question Paul is addressing here: Should we go on sinning so that grace increases?

Notice Paul's answer. Paul doesn't engage in doubletalk or threaten punishment of any kind or loss of salvation here. Instead, here's a paraphrase of how he answers their concern: "What? Are you crazy? How can we as new creations and slaves of righteousness even think of continuing in sin? It's nearly impossible! You people sound like you have no clue what actually happened to you at salvation! Do you not even realize that you went through a radical surgery at the core of your being? You died with Jesus. You were buried with Jesus. Then you were raised with Jesus to newness of life. So how in the world do you even think you can continue with sinning? You're going to hate it. You have a new default setting. You're addicted to righteousness. Continuing long-term in the same sinful choices is nearly an impossibility given that your sinful heart was ripped out and replaced with an obedient heart. Now that you have presented yourselves to God and have become new at the core, the most logical thing in the world is for you to present your bodies to Him too. Anything less and trust me—you will be miserable!"

WHAT GOD IS SAYING

Elsewhere, Paul equates our becoming righteous to Jesus's becoming sin: "He made Him who knew no sin to be sin on our behalf, so that *we might become the righteousness of God in Him*" (2 Corinthians 5:21).

Did Jesus really become sin on the cross? Yes. Certainly, we would take Paul at his word on that. Similarly, we *really* became righteous. Notice how Paul expresses it: We became the righteousness of God. This leaves little to the imagination about just how righteous we are and whether it is real or not. "We are the righteousness of God" means that we are *as righteous as God*. The quality of our righteousness is the same as God's. In fact, God's righteousness is *who we have become*. Wow, now that is something to think about more deeply!

It's not just the apostles John and Paul who want to convince us of a real and internal righteousness we possess. Peter says we are "partakers of the divine nature" (2 Peter 1:4) and we've been "born again not of seed which is perishable but imperishable" (1 Peter 1:23). One has to ask: "If I partake of the divine nature, and I'm born of God's imperishable seed, then what does that say about me? My nature? My self? My heart? My righteousness?"

Maybe God is trying to tell you something.

PERFECT GOD, PERFECT YOU

You can't say you're born of God but not really righteous. You can't say you're born of the Spirit but not really righteous. That's a contradiction.

Once we confront this sort of contradiction in our belief system, we can understand our new identity in Christ at a whole new level. We can see more fully that the new birth is a real transformation that occurred at the core of our being and that our passions and desires (what we really want) have actually changed.

We are literally slaves of righteousness.

After all, if the Spirit of God gave birth to you, then what kind of person was born? What kind of spiritual DNA was shared with you? Through spiritual rebirth, your goodness is directly tied to the goodness of God: *Not believing that your new-hearted self is now entirely good is equivalent to believing that God isn't entirely good either.*

God, the Giver of All Good Gifts, has given you your new-hearted self: the perfect you. God, the Giver of Eternal Life, gave birth to you: the perfect you. So what kind of self did He give you? What kind of person did He give birth to? Who exactly was born the day you believed?

PART 4

THE PERFECT STORM

CHAPTER 9

I magine you get a new phone—shiny, untouched, and perfect. You lift it out of the box with awe and can't wait to use it. It'll be so much better than your old one!

Yet even the newest, shiniest hardware (like your phone) still requires software updates. And if you ignore those update requests and keep it running on older software, pretty soon you'll notice problems. It will slow down, some things won't work, and you'll keep getting reminders that there's something wrong.

It's much the same with your life in Christ. You have shiny new "heartware," but you still need software updates—the renewing of your mind. As you make your way around the planet every day, have you noticed you're getting offers for software updates from the God of the Universe? Yes, God is offering software updates to your mind that are perfectly compatible with your heart.

Now let's get technical. Here's what's so great about those software updates: They aren't downloads from Heaven, but rather "uploads" from your heart to your head. But sometimes you delay the inevitable, don't you? You might just click the option for "Remind me later, Lord."

But here's the all-important distinction: Even though your unrenewed mindsets are like out-of-date software, you *already have* new spiritual heartware. The software updates are a process. They're progressive. But you have the full set of new heartware right here and now.

There's no waiting.

You have the obedient heart already. God cleaned house and moved in. He doesn't live in dirty places. You're like the Holy of Holies. You're a temple of the Holy Spirit.

Together—the perfect you and the perfect God—are a perfect fit!

Our Battle with Software

But software updates are desperately needed! Let's face it: If you're anything like us, you're inundated with thoughts—critical thoughts, lustful thoughts, embarrassing thoughts. Not knowing the source, you imagine the thoughts are coming from you. Then the religious world offers up a statement about your being "desperately wicked." And it's all confirmed.

But here's a freeing, life-giving truth: That out-of-date software isn't really you. You are the shiny new heartware. The outdated software running in your mind is like memories of old coping mechanisms from the world that you once used to make life work. This is what the Bible calls *the flesh*. And the battle with the flesh is real.

Get this, though: You're *not* the flesh. You're a child of God. It's not a "good half" of you versus a "bad half" of you. You don't have two hearts. You don't have two selves or two spiritual natures.

Who you are is entirely—100 percent—the new self. The fight is against the world, fleshly thinking, and the enemy. There *is* a war within the believer, but it's not a civil war. You are not your own worst enemy. Remember that it makes no sense to call yourself a friend of God and your own worst enemy at the same time.

But the battle is real. It takes place every single day. It's not easy. You get the thoughts—the greedy thoughts, the prideful thoughts, the angry thoughts. They come in so many flavors. But it does make a difference if you recognize that *those thoughts don't come from your new-hearted self.* And God would never speak to you that way!

Sinful thoughts don't originate from within any part of who you are. You are the new self with a new heart, a new spirit, and God's Spirit. You don't desire to sin at your core. So let your heart beat and let it beat strongly. Don't let it skip a single beat. Allow it to be fully expressed at all times.

Think about it: If sin is who you are and what you want, then good luck saying "no" to yourself for decades on end until you hit Heaven. But if you're on God's team and the thoughts are not from you, this simple revelation can be a tremendous relief in itself.

You're called to a whole new way of interpreting your thought life. When a sinful thought travels down the hallway of your mind—a lustful thought, a gossipy thought, a hateful thought—you're invited to say, "I count myself dead to this thought and alive to you, God. This thought did not originate with me, and it does not fit with who I am."

TAKE IT TO HEART

Why do you so often fail to believe you're new-hearted? Most likely it's because of your most recent version of *thinking*. When you take a survey of the thoughts that have infiltrated your mind lately, you decide you can't possibly be as new as God says you are. You essentially ask yourself: *If I'm so new, then why are these thoughts even here?*

But there's a solid explanation for your thinking patterns: an unrenewed mind. This is why not every thought you entertain is trustworthy. But this in no way takes away from the reality of your new heart. You do have a go-to place within you that you can trust.

This means that when temptation hits, you don't have to shout prayers up to Heaven, waiting for some new inspiration to make its way down. Instead, you can take that simple, one-foot journey from head to heart. You can look into your heart where Christ dwells and fully live from there.

F-L-E-S-H, NOT S-E-L-F

So why do you still sin? Because you're stuck with what the Bible calls "the flesh" (Greek: *sarx*).

But the flesh is *not* your self. And the flesh is not your spiritual nature. Remember, the flesh is the patterns and pathways of worldly thinking that you sometimes adopt. So walking according to the flesh disagrees with your new self. And walking according to God's Spirit is in perfect harmony with the new you.

For many years, the term "sinful nature" was used as a substitute for "flesh" (*sarx*) in the New International Version. As a result, many believers thought they had one good nature and one sinful nature. Many used this duality to define their fight against temptation. They literally imagined one part of themselves (new nature) fighting against another part of themselves (sinful nature).

After decades, the NIV committee changed most instances of *sarx* to its literal translation "flesh." This is a big deal. It's always better to use the actual words—like "flesh," "sin," and "new self"—that we find in the Bible to define our struggle. Otherwise, we can end up with a skewed view of what we're actually experiencing when a sinful thought hits us. But here's a fun way to remember the truth, given that so many believers have read the situation "backwards":

Our real problem is the F-L-E-S-H, not the S-E-L-F.

Too many people have literally ended up with a "backward theology" by believing S-E-L-F to be the problem instead of F-L-E-S-H. For the believer, the flesh and the self are true opposites in every way. The flesh opposes your self. Your self opposes the flesh.

THE PROBLEM IS NOT YOU

In a good sermon, we hear "Your old self died," but days later we find ourselves saying, "My problem is my self. I keep letting my self get in the way."

Do we even see the contradiction? The whole time, God is thinking, "You're the new self. How could your new and only self get in My way?"

What if God is trying to show you something beautiful that is the polar opposite of what man-made religion might tell you? What if God is trying to show you your perfect self, and all this time you've been holding on to a lesser message instead?

PLAY THE GAME!

Let's suppose you decide to buy the idea that your opponent is the flesh and not your self. Then what? Do you wake up every day and try to analyze flesh patterns in your thought life in order to avoid them?

It's healthy to recognize the old ways you've been thinking compared to the new ways God is teaching you now. But in terms of your focus each day, you should not be analyzing the flesh. Instead, you're invited to a much simpler and more uplifting focus:

> But I say, **walk by the Spirit**, and you will **not** carry out the desire of the flesh. (Galatians 5:16)

Notice the solution is *not* analysis or introspection. It's putting your focus on God's Spirit. Scripture tells us to forget what lies behind (don't harp on failures!) and press on (Philippians 3:13), fixing our eyes on Jesus (Hebrews 12:2).

Focusing on what lies in the past, on the failures of the flesh, will just frustrate and discourage us. There's a good reason God has told us that He's forgotten our sins and remembers them no more: He doesn't want us focused there.

If you're petrified by a fear of failure, constantly analyzing, "Is this flesh or is this Spirit?", it will paralyze you. You become your own judge and jury and counselor. It's too much to bear.

Imagine playing a basketball game. You're dribbling the ball down the court, but every few seconds you stop to see if the referee has blown the whistle or not. How effective of a player are you? After a few minutes of this, the coach pulls you off the court and says, "Just play the game! When the ref blows the whistle, you'll hear it. In the meantime, play your heart out!"

That's exactly what God's saying to you—play the game, live your life. Walk by the Spirit. Focus on Jesus. God is big enough to "blow the whistle" and bring up an issue if it needs to be addressed. Until then, keep walking in dependence on the indwelling Christ and "play the game." Or as the Apostle Paul put it—run the race.

EXAMINING OURSELVES

The idea of regularly examining yourself is common in Christian circles. Examining yourself, your heart, and your recent track record may feel humble, self-effacing, and religious. But is it scriptural?

Even under the Old Covenant, David says, "Search me, O God" (Psalm 139:23). David doesn't search himself. He knows God serves as the Counselor and Guide into all truth.

And under the New Covenant, the Apostle Paul writes this surprising passage:

> *But to me it is a very small thing that I may be examined by you, or by any human court; in fact, **I do not even examine myself**. For I am conscious of nothing against myself, yet I am not by this acquitted; but **the one who examines me is the Lord**.* (1 Corinthians 4:3–4)

Apparently, conducting your own spiritual self-inspection is *not* what you're called to do! Until otherwise notified by the God of the Universe, you can assume everything is on track. And even when an issue arises, continue to trust Christ to guide you through it. The answer is always Him:

> *You will keep in perfect peace all who trust in you, **all whose thoughts are fixed on you!*** (Isaiah 26:3 NLT)

Experiencing peace comes from fixing your thoughts on Christ, not on your own performance or on the flesh. Another way to think of it is like this: You don't walk into a dark room and cast out darkness. You simply turn on the light.

Jesus is our light. We look to Him. There's no condemnation for us, as we are totally forgiven anyway. So we don't need to be fixated on the flesh and foster a sin-consciousness rather than a Christ-consciousness. Jesus is *always* the focus.

Chapter 10

J esus said a house divided against itself cannot stand (Matthew 12:25). Fortunately, you're *not* a house divided. You aren't two people. You don't have two hearts. You don't have two selves.

Yes, the battle is very real. The fight is daily, and the struggle is obvious. But the battle is not against your own self. You're united with Christ, and you're on God's team.

The old software known as "the flesh" is completely untrustworthy. Don't trust it. And don't trust the world or the enemy. Don't trust them.

But you are *not* them.

You're the new self, and you *can* trust what God has done in you.

FAILURE AND ACCUSATION

What happens when you fail?

Those old mindsets of law-based religion are waiting to pounce on you. "Of course, you failed," they tell you, "because you're a failure." "Of course, you sinned," they say, "because you're a dirty sinner by nature."

But that voice isn't God. It's not the Spirit speaking to you. That's the Accuser operating through your old belief system (the flesh) to shame you. The premise is that you are what you do. And remember: That's not the truth that sets you free!

Today, when you fail under God's grace, here's what God's Spirit has to say to your spirit: "You failed, but you are no failure. You sinned, but that's out of character for you. You acted like someone you're not. Remember who you are. Be who you are. And as far as any repair with others that's needed, we will walk through this together."

This is the voice of the Comforter, the Counselor, and the Guide into all truth. This is God's protective wisdom that works with your heart, not against it, to direct you away from the harm of sin.

TWO TYPES OF PROGRAMMING

Today, Americans are divided politically, maybe more than ever. This seems to be reflected in the press as well. Turn to one TV station, and you can nearly guarantee they'll be criticizing the president within minutes. Turn to another TV station, and they're nearly always praising the president. The same events are happening, but the two perspectives on those events are wildly different.

There's a similar phenomenon when it comes to your own mind. It seems there are two stations being broadcast at the same time. On one station, you're being told that you're nothing more than a product of your upbringing. You're defined by your past, whether it be filled with failure, success, abuse, or affirmation. Your background and environment tell you your comparative worth. As you listen to this programming, strongholds in your thinking are developed. You begin to believe that your identity is your guilt, your shame, or even your self-effort and worldly success.

On the other station, you're being invited to embrace the new-hearted, perfect you. You're being urged to look beyond your knee-jerk reactions, your old habits, and your current thinking patterns. There's even instruction about where the accusatory and shameful thoughts really come from. You're being told that your heart is new and clean and filled with Jesus. Ultimately, you're being called to learn who you really are and then wake up every day and be yourself.

DEBORAH CHANGED THE STATION

Deborah had experienced extreme treatment growing up. She was sexually abused by her father and one of her brothers. When she told her mom about it, her cries were ignored, and her concerns were dismissed. The message Deborah received was that she was worth less than the men in her family. She began to believe that she was totally *worthless* and started contemplating suicide. Eventually, she tried to take her life, but she seemed to be a failure at that too.

One day, she heard our message on "the perfect you" and discovered her new identity in Christ. She learned that she was not the sum total of her past and that the messages she had received from her parents about herself did not determine her true worth or value. She began taking in the truth of who God says she is, and she started to dismiss the enemy's lies about her.

In short, she changed the station.

Maybe you're like Deborah with a past full of negative messages about yourself and where you "rank" in comparison with those around you. Or maybe you are nothing like Deborah. Your past may be filled with success stories and affirmations. Either way, it makes little difference if you are deriving your self-image from surroundings and achievements (or lack thereof). All the while, your new heart will be tugging at you to move in this direction:

> *And do not be conformed to this world, but **be transformed by the renewing of your mind**, so that you may prove what the will of God is, that which is good and acceptable and perfect.* (Romans 12:2)

God wants to renew your mind to who you really are. Along the way, there will be important decisions to make. First, you'll need to be *adamant* about seeking God's view of you, because *His view is reality.* Second, you'll need to "change the channel," sometimes again and again, when it comes to the incoming messages about you. You might think you should entertain the accusations, wrestle with them, engage and defend yourself against them. But God wants you to *ignore* them:

> *Even so **consider yourselves to be dead to sin**, but alive to God in Christ Jesus. Therefore **do not let sin reign** in your mortal body so that you obey **its** lusts.* (Romans 6:11–12)

It's okay to just change the channel. You don't have to analyze or inspect the thoughts that sin offers you. Why are you getting such sinful thoughts? Don't be surprised. The power of sin is capable of offering any believer any thought of any kind at any time.

That's all there is to it. Sure, you could inspect things further and land on theories as to why a particular pattern of thoughts is plaguing you specifically. But this assumes that analysis is going to lead to better resistance, and many times this is simply not the case.

We know lots of people who have analyzed and shared the nature of their struggles quite well and yet continue to struggle just as much. God seems to be telling us that we can just choose to ignore a lie, fuel up on the truth, and move along without further question as to the "why" of a sinful thought.

MICHAEL WAS SCARED

A man named Michael once wrote us an email to express his fear of the sinful thoughts he was receiving:

I am thankful for the message of God's grace, and I know it to be true more and more. But I still keep looking back at my past, and I can't seem to shake my past failures, my current lust from the flesh, and fear of screwing up in the future. The thoughts come at the most inopportune times, it seems. It's hard to be with my wife and not have a thought from something in my past or the flesh, and I hate it. What's worse is she knows it, and it kills her.

Michael was getting hammered with temptation and accusation all at once. And the power of sin was happy to bring it to him in the most inconvenient scenarios. While seeking to be intimate with his wife, Michael's mind would be flooded with old thoughts and images from past relationships. Then he'd get hit with accusation: "I can't believe you're thinking about those women! What kind of Christian husband are you?"

Michael was so bombarded with the thoughts that he sought relief by telling his wife about them. This provided him no relief and hurt his wife deeply because she felt compared to those past relationships.

But what if Michael knew those thoughts didn't come from him? What if he knew the thoughts did not represent his heart or his true desires? Might he then take less "ownership" of them and more readily dismiss them as *interference* that any Christian can get at any time? (After all, how many of us have been minding our own business and gotten hit with random sinful thoughts out of the blue?)

Furthermore, what if Michael's wife knew her identity in Christ (and Michael's identity too!), and they could both recognize that they share *a common enemy*—the power of sin? If that's where the thoughts are coming from, they can agree they're still on the same team as husband and wife—not enemies—in the moment the thoughts arrive.

Here's part of an email that we wrote to Michael as encouragement:

> Those are not your thoughts. They do not originate with you. The enemy wants to try to humiliate you or make you feel embarrassed or ashamed of the thought that you received in that moment. But it is not from you. Sin is masquerading as you and then accusing you. You can feel free to ignore the thought completely and not be surprised that it was offered. The enemy wants you to make it into a big deal. Just because you received the thought doesn't mean it's yours or that it came from you. Count yourself dead to the thought and just move on. Don't take in accusation or guilt over the thought being presented. You can't control what thoughts come at you. You can only decide what you will do with them.

YOUR DEFAULT SETTING

You are called to a whole new way of thinking. When a sinful thought travels down the hallway of your mind—a lustful thought, a gossipy thought, a critical thought—you're called to say, "I count myself dead to this thought, and I am alive to you, God. Sin does not fit with who I am."

After all, if a sinful thought fit with who you are, then you would be doomed to eventually think it, entertain it, and milk it for all it's worth. You'd have to wait until Heaven to have any victory over it. But the truth is that what you're experiencing is simply the "stinking thinking" flesh patterns from your past as they replay in your brain, sometimes accompanied by a special dose of shame from the Accuser.

Here's another way to express it: Computers come from the factory with certain default settings on them. What we're saying is that your default setting is now righteousness. Sin goes against who you are. Sin is just weird for you. And when you believe any differently, you're being duped.

Yes, we know you've been told (and can even feel!) the opposite—that you *want* to sin and that it's more difficult to do the "right" thing. And we do get that there's resistance from the flesh and the world around you. But can we talk about your true heartfelt desire?

You're a slave of righteousness (Romans 6:17–18). You can't get away from it. As a new creation, you want what God wants, whether you like it or not. (And you do like it!)

CHAPTER 11

We've discussed the flesh and sinful temptation to some degree. Now let's put the pieces together to get a clearer picture of what you're experiencing when the thoughts come at you.

You're very familiar with your body. You look in the mirror and see it every day. Its five senses help you connect to the world around you through seeing, hearing, smelling, touching, and tasting. You feed it, exercise it, and give it rest. And it changes—growing as you move from childhood to adulthood, always aging over time.

You're also familiar with your soul. It's your personality and where your thoughts and feelings are experienced. And each one of us has a unique one!

But did you know that you also have a spirit? Here, we don't mean God's Spirit—your spirit! Yes, the Bible says you are made up of three parts—spirit, soul, and body (1 Thessalonians 5:23). This sketch can help you visualize how God made you:

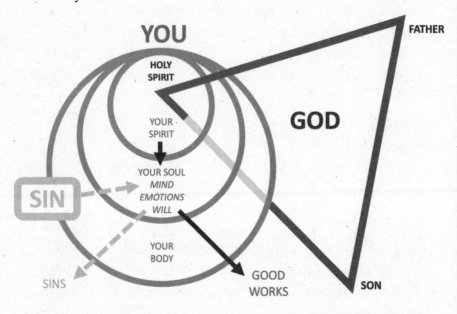

The New Testament doesn't always make a distinction between spirit and soul. Sometimes we are simply described as having an "inner man" (invisible part—spirit and soul together) and an "outer man" (visible part—body). But the author of Hebrews says there's a difference between soul and spirit, and God can show us that difference:

> *For the word of God is living and active and sharper than any two-edged sword, and piercing as far as **the division of soul and spirit,** of both joints and marrow, and able to judge the thoughts and intentions of the heart.* (Hebrews 4:12)

YOUR HUMAN SPIRIT

Your human spirit (Greek: *pneuma*) is the centermost part of you. Your spirit is what sets you apart from the animal kingdom, and it's how you relate to God. Jesus said those who worship God do so *in spirit* and in truth (John 4:24).

It's important to recognize that your human spirit is different from the Holy Spirit. As an unbeliever, you had a human spirit that was dead to God and alive to sin. At salvation, your old spirit was crucified and buried with Christ. It's now gone. And then a new human spirit was given to you through the resurrection of Christ. Your new human spirit is alive to God and dead to sin.

Your new human spirit is where Christ dwells within you. This doesn't mean that you lose your distinctness and become a "Jesus clone." It simply means that the unique spiritual you is joined to the Lord. Your new spiritual self is as close to God as you can be:

> *Jesus answered and said to him, "If anyone loves Me, he will keep My word; and My Father will love him, and **We will come to him and make Our abode with him."*** (John 14:23)

> *Or do you not know that the one who joins himself to a prostitute is one body with her? For He says, "The two shall become one flesh." But **the one who joins himself to the Lord is one spirit with Him.*** (1 Corinthians 6:16–17)

Notice the triangle in the diagram on page 98. This represents the presence of God with you and in you: Father, Son, and Holy Spirit. At salvation, you are connected to God through your spirit at the very core of your being. The entire Trinity is happy to have you (John 14:23). Your spirit is a perfect fit with God's Spirit, and you are bonded together with Him forever.

YOUR SOUL, EXPLAINED

Next, there's your soul. Your soul (Greek: *psuché*) is your psychology or your personality. It includes your mind, your will, and your emotions. This is where you think, choose, and feel.

Your soul is much like a mirror because it can "reflect" anything at a given moment. Your soul is designed to reflect your core (your spirit), but you don't always choose to let it reflect your core. Often, your soul reflects those old patterns of thinking and reacting when you choose what you're offered by the flesh.

When your soul reflects something that's not from your core, this is called "setting your mind on the flesh" and "walking by the flesh." Conversely, when your soul reflects your spirit, this is called "setting the mind on the Spirit" and "walking by the Spirit."

"FLESH" DOES NOT MEAN "BODY"

It's important to understand here that "setting your mind on the flesh" and "walking by the flesh" do not mean yielding to your supposedly "evil" body. No, there's nothing spiritually bad about your human body. God says your body is "holy and acceptable" to Him, and it is His temple (Romans 12:1; 1 Corinthians 6:19). So your body is not your opponent. No, "the flesh" here refers to the following:

- A worldly way to set the mind (Romans 8:5–6; Colossians 3:2)
- A worldly way to walk (Romans 8:4; Galatians 5:16)
- Worldly ways that include immorality, angry outbursts, jealousy, and disputes (Galatians 5:19–21)

This last passage from Galatians 5 helps us understand "the flesh" better. It's not your body that gets angry. Your body doesn't get jealous or argue with others. So clearly, "the flesh" here means something different from your physical body. "The flesh" refers to the old thinking and behavior patterns—the worldly ways you learned (and still learn) to react while not trusting Christ.

YOUR SOUL CAN CHOOSE

There's a battle at the gateway of your soul. There are decisions to be made.

Your spirit is new, but your soul is where thinking and actions progressively become more consistent with who you *already* are. This is absolutely key. It's not that you need to become something you're not. It's that your soul—when not deceived by outside influencers—can "reflect" more and more of who you already are.

When do you "set the mind on the flesh" or "walk by the flesh"? This happens when you choose (in your soul) to believe a lie about God or about who He has made you to be. When you believe you are sinful, you choose to reflect the worldly, fleshly ways of sin. For example, when you believe in a particular moment that you are a lustful or jealous person, you buy the lie, act in a way that's contrary to who you really are, and then experience godly regret over it.

But when you choose to believe who you are in a given moment, you can act as a true expression of Jesus. For example, when you make the choice to forgive and release someone rather than harboring bitterness, you experience confirmation (a knowing, not always a feeling) that your decision to forgive was what you really wanted.

It's important to note that your spiritual connection with God is never lost, no matter how you might think or walk. You're always *in* the Spirit, even though you don't always choose to *walk by* the Spirit:

> *If we **live** by the Spirit, let us also **walk** by the Spirit.* (Galatians 5:25)

THE SOURCE OF SINFUL THOUGHTS

At this point, maybe you're wondering, "If I'm truly a new creation, then where do all these sinful thoughts originate from? I know there are old, fleshly thinking patterns stored away in my brain, but it also seems like I can get any thought—even new and nasty thoughts—that can penetrate my mind without warning. They sure feel like me, and they even sound like me! Are you saying they aren't me?"

Yes, that's exactly what we're saying! They're not coming from you.

You may be thinking, "But they sound exactly like me. In fact, I'm pretty sure they are me!"

We know that's what they sound like. But they're not really you at all. The Bible makes it clear that sinful thoughts don't originate with you. They come from a parasitic power called sin:

> No longer am I the one doing it, but sin which dwells in me. (Romans 7:17b)

> I am no longer the one doing it, but sin which dwells in me. (Romans 7:20b)

Romans 7 is a landmark passage on the human struggle with sin under the Law. No matter the view one takes of it (whether Paul was describing his experience as a believer or as a devout Pharisee), the takeaway is still the same: A parasitic power called sin was enslaving him, and he was out of control. You can interpret this to be an unbeliever who was a "slave of sin," or to be a believer experiencing sin of every kind. Either way, the point is that a parasitic power called sin was at the root of the problem.

This power called sin is not a verb (like *sinning*) but is instead a noun—a thing. *Vine's Complete Expository Dictionary of Old and New Testament Words* explains that this power called sin (Greek: *hamartia*) is a "governing principle or power" that is "personified," and it is "an organized power, acting through the members of the body."

So let's put this together and make it personal: *A power called "sin" has person-like characteristics and—through organized strategies—offers thoughts to my brain. Very easily, I might think these thoughts are coming from me, but they're not!*

The Power (Sin) and the Pathway (Flesh)

In the spirit-soul-body diagram, the temptations brought on by this power called sin are illustrated with dashed lines. The dashes represent the fact that these sinful messages come from a source *outside of who you are.* They come from sin, and *you are not sin.*

In contrast, notice that the messages from your spirit (where you're unified with God's Spirit) are shown as solid lines. Why? Because messages from God are truth-filled, and they're *consistent with who you are.*

When you choose sin, you're acting like someone else. When you choose dependence on Christ, you're truly acting like yourself.

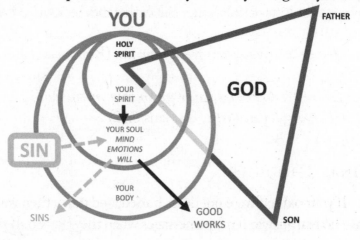

Take note of where the power called "sin" is in the dia-gram: halfway in your body and halfway in the world. Sin came into the world at the Fall, so it is all around you. But this power of sin also has access to you through the brain. The power of sin fires thoughts at you, and typically these thoughts align with how you've been deceived in the past.

Lastly, the flesh—the old, worldly mindsets—are the dashed lines themselves. These are *the pathways of thought* that you've often visited over time. This is precisely why you need the renewing of your mind over time. You have those old habits and patterns of thinking (Romans 12:2).

So, when it comes to temptation, *sin is the power* and *the flesh is the pattern or pathway.* But you are not sin, and you are not the flesh. They are your opponents, not part of who you are.

The fact that your "soul mirror" sometimes reflects the flesh and sin doesn't mean you should identify with those thoughts. They are not you. In those moments, you're acting like someone you're not. And because you died to sin's power and were raised up to new life in Christ, you've been freed to say *no* to the lusts of sin. Notice below that they're not *your* lusts!

*For he who has died is **freed** from sin.* (Romans 6:7)

*Therefore **do not let sin reign** in your mortal body so that you obey **its lusts**.* (Romans 6:12)

Final Thoughts

If your old self were not dead, buried, and gone, then you'd have no real answer for sin's messages when they hit you. If you were in the process of dying to sin, then when temptation hit, perhaps you'd only be 42 percent dead to its power.

So, is the good news of the Gospel that you have a 42 percent chance of saying "no" to sin? Do you need to wait on some further death or some sort of "fix" before you're ready to resist temptation? No, you can count yourself 100 percent dead to sin and fully alive to God "once for all." Because of your co-crucifixion and co-resurrection with Christ, you are just as dead to sin as Jesus Himself (Romans 6:10–11). This is how you enjoy the capacity to say "no" to sin right now.

That persistent temptation to watch pornography hits you, and you're ready to say "no" right away. Waiting for more spiritual growth is not necessary. You are dead to that thought right now. Memories of past abuse flood your mind, telling you they define you and that you're worthless. You're ready to say "no" to those thoughts too, right away. Waiting for more maturity or more understanding is not necessary. God has made you dead to sin "once for all" (Romans 6:10–11), so that you can enjoy freedom from nagging temptation in any and every moment. This is a huge benefit to the finished work of the cross. Your death to sin is over. You are permanently allergic to sin and addicted to Jesus. It's who you are!

PART 5

THE PERFECT FIT

Chapter 12

L et's talk a little more about *your soul.*

Some think that, after salvation, your soul is progressively getting better, cleaner. They say the soul is, little by little, being made ready for Heaven. Is this the case?

There's no passage in the New Testament that says we'll receive a last-minute "soul polish" just as we arrive at the Pearly Gates. For that reason, we don't believe the soul is partly clean and partly dirty right now.

All too often, though, we've seen people fight for the truth that our old self died and that we're an entirely new self now, only to turn right around and say that our spirit *is* clean, but our soul is "getting clean." In so doing, they exchange one "civil war" of personhood for another. In other words, they simply exchange one "house divided" (old self versus new self) for another "house divided" (spirit versus soul).

The truth is that *your soul is Heaven-ready.*

Think about it. God hasn't declared that He'll take your spirit to Heaven but not your personality (soul). If Jesus were to return in this moment, or if you were to die physically right now, your soul would go with your spirit to Heaven. And God's not waiting at Heaven's entrance with a "soul squeegee" as you walk in. No, your soul is Heaven-ready right now.

Your Heaven-Ready Soul

How is your soul Heaven-ready but still involved in sinful choices on Earth? Remember that your soul is like a mirror. Every moment here on Earth, you have a choice: Will you let your soul *reflect* your new, God-given self, or will you let it *reflect* the flesh? Either way, there's nothing intrinsically wrong with the mirror.

Put another way, your soul is like a room with two door-ways. One doorway has a set of wide-open double doors going from your spirit to your soul. These doors stay open all the time. Then there's another smaller door across the room that gives access to thoughts from the flesh and from the outside world.

When you choose to open the door to the outside world, anything might blow in for a time. It could be a sinful thought, a false belief, or an accusation. But just because a piece of trash blows in from the street doesn't mean the room itself is designed for trash. Sometimes you temporarily house a thought in the soul that *doesn't define the soul or give the soul a nature.*

But in Heaven, the "trash" from the world and the flesh and sin are gone forever. Put another way, your soul mirror can only reflect righteousness there, because that's all that's left. In Heaven, those old flesh patterns (currently stored in your brain) will be completely gone. They'll be left behind in the coffin! In short, your soul will only reflect your spirit.

THERE'S NOTHING WRONG WITH YOU!

Your soul is an "experiencer." You can experience anything in the soul, *but there's nothing wrong with the soul itself.* While your soul can *experience* anything, it doesn't have a spiritual nature. And while the experience of your soul here on Earth can definitely get better as you learn the joys of reflecting your true self, your soul itself is not getting "better." Instead, it is simply fulfilling its designed purpose, more and more, by having truer experiences.

This is why it's wrong to imagine yourself going to Heaven with a 67 percent clean soul that needs a last-minute carwash. This is never stated in Scripture. And that's why it's wrong for us to regard the soul as dirty or sinful.

The mirror is not the problem; what the mirror is reflecting is the problem.

In other words, the influencers known as sin and the flesh are dirty and sinful, but you are not. "Self" is not a dirty word for Christians, and neither is "soul." Notice that in Scripture, when God tells you that you're holy and righteous and blameless, He is not speaking to a spiritual compartment of you, but to you as a whole.

So what's the big takeaway here? There's *nothing* wrong with who you are!

God does not merely accept a portion of you. Your spirit is set apart and acceptable to God. Your soul is set apart and acceptable to God. And even your body is set apart and acceptable to God.

You can find nearly anyone who will accept bits and pieces of you. But you don't have to worry about that with God. You can be yourself. He truly gives you the freedom to be you as He embraces every part of you.

The Renewing of Your Mind

If your soul is not dirty or sinful, then what about the renewing of your mind? Doesn't that mean that your soul (which houses your mind) is somehow tainted? After all, Romans says this about the mind:

> *And do not be conformed to this world, but **be transformed by the renewing of your mind**, so that you may prove what the will of God is, that which is good and acceptable and perfect.* (Romans 12:2)

You're learning, and you're growing. Your mind is being renewed, for sure. But the fact that you don't know everything and that you have so much to learn (and unlearn!) doesn't mean your soul is inherently dirty or sinful. Even Jesus grew in wisdom and stature (Luke 2:52). And He learned obedience over time:

*Although He was a Son, **He learned obedience** from the things which He suffered.* (Hebrews 5:8)

Jesus learned and grew, and it was not a threat to His righteousness. Likewise, you learn and grow, but this doesn't mean you're less righteous on Monday than you are on Tuesday. You'll continue to learn and grow throughout all of eternity, even with a perfect resurrection body!

WHAT ABOUT YOUR BODY?

Finally, if your spirit and your soul are 100 percent acceptable to God, then what about your body? Isn't your body sinful?

While a group of early church heretics known as Gnostics might agree with that idea, God says the polar opposite. He tells you to present your body to Him every day as a holy and righteous instrument:

> *And do not go on presenting the members of your body to sin as instruments of unrighteousness; **but present yourselves to God as those alive from the dead, and your members as instruments of righteousness to God.*** (Romans 6:13)

> *Therefore I urge you, brethren, by the mercies of God, **to present your bodies a living and holy sacrifice, acceptable to God,** which is your spiritual service of worship.* (Romans 12:1)

While the Gnostics essentially rejected their own physicality (or relegated it to a place of non-importance), God esteems our bodies and tells us that they're set apart for Him. This is yet another motivation for upright living in dependence on the One who transformed us.

> Or do you not know that **your body is a temple of the Holy Spirit** who is in you, whom you have from God, and that you are not your own? (1 Corinthians 6:19)

The parasite known as sin and the old behavior patterns known as the flesh can influence you. They persuade you to reflect sin with your soul (and body) rather than who you really are. But there's nothing sinful or wrong about your soul or your body in themselves.

Your body is not your enemy. Your soul is not your opponent. And your spirit isn't either. God wholly and completely embraces all of who you are. So what if there's actually nothing wrong with you?

There isn't! Welcome to *the perfect you.*

GOD'S NOT HOLDING OUT ON YOU!

Religion says, "Sin is amazingly enticing, and the world is living it up, but you're not allowed to. Stay away. You better not give in to *your* desires, or else."

God's message to us is the opposite: "Sin is amazingly damaging, and deep-down, those who pursue it are miserable. But you, My child, are *good*, through and through. You're dead to sin and alive to Me. For you, sin is awkward and unfulfilling and goes against every fiber of your being—spirit, soul, and body."

The most *unnatural* thing for you is to sin. And the most *natural* thing for you is to display Jesus. This is the plain truth about you. When you choose to walk by the flesh, all sorts of alarms go off inside you. You feel uncomfortable and unfulfilled, to say the least. You're not designed to walk by the flesh, and your "system" knows it. Walking by the Spirit is your new default setting. Everything else goes against the grain.

CHAPTER 13

I t seems like every year, increasingly dangerous wildfires
rage across California. As the winds fan the flames across
many miles, nearly everything that lies in the path of the fire
is destroyed.

Fire often represents God's presence in the Bible. When
the Holy Spirit came to indwell believers at Pentecost, tongues
of fire burned over their heads. Moses spoke to the Angel of
the Lord in a burning bush. But if you read these stories carefully, you'll notice something curious: No one and nothing
was consumed by the fire of God's presence. The presence of
the Lord was like a fire, but He did not consume either the
bush or the people on whom the flame rested.

This is a picture and reminder to us of how Christ dwells
within us today without consuming us. Contrary to what many
believe and teach, the Christian life is not "all of Christ and

none of you." It's all of you *and* all of Christ in a beautiful union together. Christ indwells you, but He does not consume you. *God does not replace you. He embraces you.*

But living in the Bible Belt, we've actually seen Christian billboards that cry, "More of Him, Less of Me!" This may appear humble, but it's actually a false humility. God is not trying to diminish you before He can "use" you. To the contrary, the Gospel message is that Christ has united Himself *with* you. He wants you in dynamic partnership. So, God does not invite you to "more of Him and less of you." Remember that He already had *all* of Him and *none* of you. For eternity past, it was Him and only Him. In the Gospel, He's now inviting all of you—the new creation—to participate with all of Him.

We've seen how the belief in "all of Him and none of me" leads to passivity as people "wait on God to move." They ask, "Where are you, Lord? Waiting on you, Lord." And God's response may be, "I'm already living in you. I'm ready, and you're fully equipped, so let's walk together!"

The Gospel message is not one of Christ living *instead of* you. It's Christ living *in* you and together *with* you.

So should it be Christ living through you? Or should it be you living? The answer is *yes*. It's both.

ONENESS AND UNIQUENESS

Scripture never depicts you as merely a pipeline or a lifeless conduit to "transmit" Christ to others. No, it says you are *married* to Jesus:

Therefore, my brethren, you also were made to die to the
Law through the body of Christ, so that you might be
joined to another, to Him who was raised from the
dead, *in order that we might bear fruit for God.*
(Romans 7:4)

Your oneness with Jesus is likened to marriage, the oneness between a man and a woman. It almost seems inappro-
priate to make the comparison. Almost.

But in doing so, God shows you just how close you are to
the risen Christ. When you wonder if God is separated from
you or has turned away from you due to your performance,
you're asking the wrong question. Instead of asking how distant you are, you need to be asking how close you are!

The answer to that question is: You're always perfectly
one with Him. Your closeness to Him involves His being
in you and your being in Him. You are both intertwined
and inseparable.

Still, in a healthy marriage, one person's identity—their
wants, their needs, their personality—is not subsumed by
the other person. Marriage doesn't mean you live *as* your
spouse; rather, you live *in union* with them. You don't become
your spouse, and they don't become you. However, you do
share a name, a home, and a family. You're united, but you're
also each unique.

God's salvation plan wasn't to create countless identical
"Jesus clones" throughout history. No, you are a unique and
special living canvas on which the Master Painter paints the
brushstrokes of His life. You are His workmanship:

*For **we are His workmanship**, created in Christ Jesus
for good works, which God prepared beforehand so that
we would walk in them.* (Ephesians 2:10)

Even the Greek word *poiema* used in this verse conveys
the idea of being God's special creation or handiwork. The
Master Painter has never expressed Himself through someone
like you before in all of human history. This is a first for Him,
because only *you* are you!

God cherishes your personality, your sense of humor, and
all that sets you apart from other people. So it isn't Christ
instead of you, and it isn't Christ *as* you. It's Christ *and* you.

YOU'RE NOT A FIREHOSE!

So you're not a "firehose" through whom God wants to
flow. You're a child of God in intimate relationship with Jesus.
To say you must be diminished in any way is to say that you're
not qualified or that you don't fit with Jesus because you must
be pushed down or changed first. That's rejection, whether
it's dressed up in religious jargon or not.

After all, how are those ideas any different from world
religions that teach self-abasement? They claim a follower
must get rid of themselves, or at least get themselves out of
the way so a higher state can be achieved where it's all God,
or all "divine light," and not them.

As we'll discover, there's a lot of Christian jargon and
many misinterpretations of the Bible that lead people to
believe all kinds of morbid things about themselves and God.

SELF-DESTRUCT?

Have you ever heard someone say something like this?

- "You need to get out of the way so God can work in your life."
- "God is humbling you so you will surrender."
- "God is breaking you so He can use you."
- "You need to deny yourself, die to self, and die daily like Paul did."

These messages sound very religious. They appear to elevate God as they push you down. But are they the truth that sets you free?

No, they're actually not.

Instead, they discourage you. They can scare you. And ultimately, they put you under a religious bondage that says you're not acceptable. They don't merely tell you that you need to "do more" and "be more" like so many legalistic messages out there. No, while slinging around just a bit of convincing Christianese, they actually insist you must participate in self-mutilation, the destruction of your very self.

But remember that you're not an obstacle to God. You're His instrument!

SURRENDER?

Let's talk about surrender. One way we can diminish the beauty of the Gospel message is by believing that God wants us to "surrender" to Him. Of course, we do depend on Christ and trust Him in everything. But for many believers, "surrendering to God"—a concept that doesn't appear anywhere in the New Testament—implies something very different.

We typically "surrender" to an enemy army when we've lost a battle. Is that what we mean to convey about our relationship with God? When we offer our bodies and ourselves to God, it's not because we have lost a struggle against Him.

Quite the opposite! We offer our bodies and ourselves to God because we're on the *same* team. We already lost our old self, and then God won our hearts forever at salvation. We want what He wants. There's no need to "surrender."

Is God Breaking You?

"Brokenness" is a trendy word in Christian circles these days. Of course, there's nothing wrong with using the word "broken" if you're referring to the world system and the way of the flesh. The world system *is* broken. The way of the flesh *is* a broken way. They don't work. Also, it's absolutely true that when you engage in worldly ways of thinking and acting, it will be painful and frustrating for you. If you look for answers in a place where there are no answers, you can expect *suffering*. Here's the difference, though: The world system is broken, but God is not breaking *you*. The way of the flesh is a broken way, but God is not breaking *you*.

We don't confess that we're broken sinners to then get saved and become broken saints! No, God is not breaking you. Instead, He is building you up in Jesus Christ (Colossians 2:7).

It's true that we *are* weak. Paul announces this himself: "But he said to me, 'My grace is sufficient for you, for my power is made perfect in *weakness*.' Therefore, I will boast all the more gladly about *my weaknesses*, so that Christ's power may rest on me" (2 Corinthians 12:9).

We are weak, but we're *not* broken. Brokenness implies the design is flawed, but we're not flawed new creations. We're righteous and whole and perfect in Christ.

Sure, we're not the source of anything. None of the fruit we bear originates from us. Christ is our source, and we're dependent creatures. But dependency is *not* brokenness. Weakness is *not* brokenness.

Sometimes these concepts can *feel* like the same thing. However, brokenness implies we're not complete or whole. But we are complete and whole, yet fully dependent at the same time. Think of it this way: Wasn't Jesus Himself complete and whole—not broken—yet dependent on the Father?

God Is Not Trying to Humble You

Here's a shocker: God is not trying to humble you. Instead, He is inviting you to humble yourself, just as Jesus did:

> *Being found in appearance as a man,* **He humbled Himself** *by becoming obedient to the point of death, even death on a cross. For this reason also,* **God highly exalted Him,** *and bestowed on Him the name which is above every name.* (Philippians 2:8–9)

Jesus *humbled Himself.* What did God do? God *exalted* Jesus. Why is this important? God wasn't looking to humble Jesus and teach Him a lesson in self-degradation. Likewise,

God the Father is not humbling you either. Here, two apostles confirm what we're saying:

> **Humble yourselves** *in the presence of the Lord, and He will* **exalt** *you.* (James 4:10)

> *Therefore* **humble yourselves** *under the mighty hand of God, that He may* **exalt** *you at the proper time.* (1 Peter 5:6)

Again, who is doing the humbling here? You are. God is not seeking to "take you down a notch." He lovingly allows you to choose to humble yourself—to recognize that He is God and you are dependent upon Him.

Real humility is not thinking less of yourself. Real humility is simply seeing yourself the way God sees you—no more and *no less.* Real humility is recognizing that you're a receiver, not a producer. You are dependent, not independent.

Everything you have—your new self, your new heart—you didn't produce, so they're not a cause for arrogance. Everything—your forgiveness, your freedom, your new life with Jesus—was given to you by God. And the fruit of receiving these incredible gifts is humility.

EARTH AT YOU. CHRIST IN YOU.

There's enough suffering in this world. We don't need to be inventing extra. If we adopt an "I'm a dirty worm" complex or an "I must be humbled" martyr syndrome, we can end up inventing extra suffering for ourselves. This mental and emotional suffering is not inflicted by God, but by our wrong belief system.

The world has plenty of suffering already for us, doesn't it? And yes, God reminds us of our dependence on Him in the midst of that suffering. But suffering comes at us from the outside, while Christ is encouraging us on the inside.

Planet Earth comes *at* you. Christ works *in* you.

Know the difference.

So have you been putting a "God label" on the painful circumstances that have been coming your way, as if He is the author of it all? God is not the author of your suffering. He is the author and perfecter of your faith.

God isn't trying to break you. He is simply revealing to you that the world system is broken. God is your Comforter and your Counselor, and He's building you up in the midst of this broken world.

CHAPTER 14

For many years, we both lived under a killjoy message. We thought we needed to cooperate with God as He "broke" us, crushed us into a fine powder, or painted us into a corner until we surrendered. We thought all of this would lead to a soul-purge of some kind, and God would be pleased.

That sort of message suppresses the peace of mind and contentment of knowing who we are right now. And there's ultimately more fear and guilt than fruit-bearing in such a message.

Why is there so little fruit?

Think about it: How can we accept other people if we don't believe God has fully accepted *us* as we are? How can we love other people if we don't believe God loves us without some serious tearing down and rebuilding?

If we only believe that God embraces a fixed-up version of us from the future, or a deep-down "spiritual" compartment of us, or a far-off "Bible view" of us, then what's the result? We will live out what we believe, and *we will seek to fix others instead of accepting them.*

Do You Need to Die to Self?

What about "dying to self"? We hear this expression often, so let's look at the Bible passages that use this expression.

Wait … we can't, because there aren't any.

What? Surely with all we hear about dying to self, there's at least one passage that uses the expression! We Christians didn't just invent that concept out of thin air, did we?

Basically, we did. (Somewhere between dying to sin, which happens at salvation and our old self dying—which also happens at salvation—we concocted the idea of "dying to self.")

The closest expression we have to "die to self" in Scripture is found in Romans 6. But there, it actually says the opposite—our old self died (past tense).

> How shall **we who died to sin** still live in it? Or do you not know that all of us who have been baptized into Christ Jesus have been baptized into His death? … knowing this, that **our old self was crucified with Him,** in order that our body of sin might be done away with, so that we would no longer be slaves to sin; for **he who has died is freed from sin.** (Romans 6:2–3, 5–6)

If it is this clear that our old self has been crucified—past tense—and we are the new self, then why are so many running around saying we need to "die to self"? Maybe it goes back to that human, religious tendency to see ourselves as an obstacle rather than an instrument.

Plus, when Romans 6 talks about our old self being crucified and buried, we weren't even the ones who did it! God did it. We *couldn't* do it. So the man-made theology of "we need to die to self every day" implies that *we do something* to rid ourselves of ourselves.

But we can't.

God chose crucifixion for good reason: It's a death that someone cannot carry out on themselves. After all, you nail one hand up. Then what?

God had to do the crucifying, burying, raising, and seating with Christ:

> *But by His doing you are in Christ Jesus,* who became to us wisdom from God, and righteousness and sanctification, and redemption. (1 Corinthians 1:30)

> *I have been crucified with Christ;* and it is no longer I who live, but Christ lives in me; and the life which I now live in the flesh I live by faith in the Son of God, who loved me and gave Himself up for me. (Galatians 2:20)

> *And [God] raised us up with Him, and seated us with Him* in the heavenly places in Christ Jesus. (Ephesians 2:6)

God crossed your heart. He took your old-hearted self to the cross. It died and was buried, never to be heard from again. Then God raised you to newness of life and unified you with Jesus. He even seated you at His right hand. You've got the best seat in the House!

This was all God's doing, and it's done. There's no need to try to "die to self" if your old self is already dead and gone. And God certainly doesn't want you trying to kill the new self.

DENY YOURSELF?

But didn't Jesus say to deny yourself, take up your cross, and follow Him (Matthew 16:24)? Yes, but He was referring to the salvation decision itself. After all, when did you take up your cross and follow Jesus to Calvary and experience death, burial, and resurrection to new life? *At salvation.*

Okay, but doesn't Luke 9:23 present a different version of the statement, saying we need to take up our cross "daily"? Actually, only a minority of Greek manuscripts contain the word "daily" in Luke 9:23, and many scholars believe the word was added as a scribal gloss—an annotation in the margin. One theory is the scribe may have had 1 Corinthians 15:31 ("I die daily") in mind as he added it. (And, yes, we'll address that passage in the next section.)

But Jesus's salvation pitch to the people surrounding Him is something every born-again believer has *already* experienced. You denied who you used to be (your old self), you took up your cross, and you followed Jesus into death. Then you awoke spiritually to a new life, being reborn of God's Spirit.

Romans 6 says your old self died with Christ. Galatians 2 says you were crucified with Him. Colossians 2 says you died with Jesus. There's no need to "die" anymore. All the dying and denying of your (old) self has already taken place. And you shouldn't be denying your new self! No, now you can *daily* count yourself dead to sin and alive to God (Romans 6:11).

"I DIE DAILY"?

Didn't Paul say "I die daily" in 1 Corinthians 15:31? Therefore, doesn't God need to scrape off the ugly parts of who you are or kill a portion of you? Then you'll become beautiful and acceptable and compatible with Him, right? If even the Apostle Paul had to die daily, surely you must too, huh?

Here, Paul is referring to the physical dangers he encountered every day as a traveling messenger of the Gospel. The dangers he refers to are persecution, arrest, and even the fact that, at one time, he "fought with wild beasts at Ephesus" (verse 32). Daily, his physical well-being was at risk.

Paul was not creating some morbid theology about your needing to spiritually die every day. The false notion that you or a part of you needs to slowly die in order to be compatible with God goes directly against the finished work of Christ.

CARRYING "THE DYING OF JESUS"?

Here's another passage that is often misconstrued to mean we still need to "die" in some way:

*But we have this treasure in earthen vessels … **always carrying about in the body the dying of Jesus,** so that the life of Jesus also may be manifested in our body.* (2 Corinthians 4:7, 10)

What does "carrying the dying of Jesus" even mean? Here's the context:

- "We [apostles] do not preach ourselves" (verse 5)
- "We [apostles] are afflicted in every way, but not crushed" (verse 8)
- "Death works in *us* [apostles] but life works in *you* [Corinthian saints]" (verses 11–12)

Paul is highlighting the physical suffering that he and his fellow apostles endured. And why did they endure it? For the benefit of the Corinthians, so that the life of Christ would manifest in more and more people. Physical death (and suffering) was at work in the apostles, but the result was life in so many others.

This passage has nothing to do with Christians needing to continually die in order to experience new life in Jesus. The apostles suffered in bringing the Gospel to many so that we can freely enjoy new life in Jesus. No dying needed!

"You Must Die"?

What about in Romans, where it says this: "For if you are living according to the flesh, *you must die*" (Romans 8:13)? Doesn't this mean that some sort of death must still take place within you?

In this chapter, Paul is distinguishing *unbelievers* from *believers*. He's saying that believers are led by the Spirit and have a new way to live. Unbelievers, on the other hand, don't have a choice. They are constantly living according to the flesh. It's all they *can* do. Therefore, they can't experience true life—only death.

Once again, we have a passage that says nothing about you as a believer needing to die. Quite the opposite: It's addressing the condition of *unbelievers* who continually experience death, now and into eternity.

SELF-ABASEMENT?

Degrading or seeking to destroy the self is a characteristic common to many man-made religions. Here's what the Apostle Paul had to say about it:

> Let no one keep defrauding you of your prize by delighting in self-abasement.... These are matters which have, to be sure, **the appearance of wisdom in self-made religion and self-abasement** and severe treatment of the body, but are of no value against fleshly indulgence. (Colossians 2:18, 23)

Here, Paul speaks of "self-abasement" as a trait of worldly religions that we should avoid. It may be tempting to think that way, but self-degradation does nothing to curb the flesh. Christianity is not about tearing you down. In the same chapter, we see God's goal is *to build you up in Jesus Christ* (Colossians 2:7).

GET BUSY LIVING!

God's not trying to break you or kill you or "fix" you in any way before He says you're okay. On a scale of one to ten, you're an eleven. You're off the charts!

If you weren't fully okay right now, how would you get that way? Thirty more visits to church? Volunteering for service work? One more year of Bible study? And how would you ever know you're finally okay? Would it be a feeling?

No, okayness (rightness with God) is a fact, not a feeling. It's not based on anything progressive, like your performance. It's based on something *finished*: Jesus's performance on the cross and His resurrection.

God likes you. God loves you. God isn't trying to break you, crush you into a fine powder, or put you on a cross (again) to crucify you. No, if you are a new creation, God doesn't need to change you in order to embrace all that you are. He already made you exactly who He wanted you to be. You're the perfect you!

PART 6

THE PERFECT ATMOSPHERE

CHAPTER 15

To this point, we've shared a lot about the perfect you. But there are other factors—beyond your own misperceptions about your spiritual self—that can contribute to missing the full beauty of who you really are as a new-hearted saint in Jesus Christ.

What about living up to God's standards? What about all the commandments I constantly break? What about God's Law? Without solid answers to these questions, you can easily be moved away from celebrating the perfect you and settle for a lesser experience.

In order to fully benefit, you must have a solid grasp, not only of the perfect you, but also of the perfect *atmosphere* God has supplied through the Gospel:

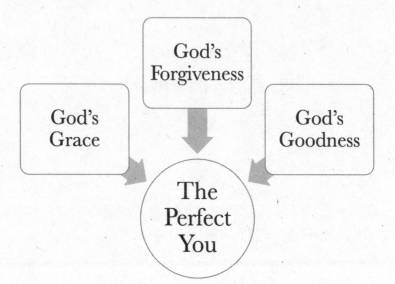

God's *grace*, God's *forgiveness*, and God's *goodness* are the perfect atmosphere in which you can best realize and most benefit from the perfect you. We turn our attention in the second half of this book to the perfect atmosphere for the perfect you to thrive in.

An Atmosphere of Grace

What kind of "atmosphere" does God offer to motivate the new-hearted you? It's an ambience of grace. Gone are the rigid requirements of law-based living. Gone is the frustration of failure and the despair of never quite measuring up.

In this new atmosphere of grace, you can be exactly who God made you. Your new heart, encouraged, starts to shine like never before. As the beautiful liberty of God's grace envelops you, you can enjoy all that He has for you.

This new atmosphere springs from a counterintuitive concept known as *the new covenant*. What do you think of when you hear the phrase "new covenant"? You might think of a church name like New Covenant Bible Church or New Covenant Chapel of God. "Covenant" isn't a word we often use these days. It sounds archaic, even obscure—and, frankly, irrelevant to our lives.

So what is the new covenant? When did it start? And why does it matter to the new-hearted you?

The New Covenant

Let's start with the word "covenant." It might sound obscure, but in fact it's a concept we use nearly every day. A covenant is a contract, a deal, or a pact. It's where two or more people or organizations come together and make an agreement with each other.

In the Bible, a covenant involving God is also referred to as a "will" or a "testament." Perhaps you've heard of a person drafting their "last will and testament" detailing what they want to happen to their assets after they die. As we'll see, it's not much different with the new covenant, which details what God wanted to leave us after Jesus's death, resurrection, and ascension.

In Hebrews 8, we learn that God made a new covenant that is totally different from the law-based covenant He had with Israel. Here's a paraphrase of what God did:

Because they did not remain faithful to Me, I decided to write my desires on their hearts and minds. I set it up so

that I will be their God, no matter what, and they will
be My people. They will all intuitively know Me, and
I will remember their sins no more. (abbreviated paraphrase of Hebrews 8:7–13)

The new covenant is essentially a *download* and a *dele-
tion*. First, God downloads His desires to your new–hearted
self. Second, He deletes your sin record and remembers it
no more!

Its True Beginning

Maybe you've heard of the concept of being "blood brothers." When we were children, we'd make promises by pricking
our fingers and then rubbing them together. It was a promise
made in blood! That idea was not birthed out of thin air. It's
loosely related to something ancient and biblical:

> *In the case of a will, it is necessary to prove the death of*
> *the one who made it, because **a will [covenant] is in***
> ***force only when somebody has died;** it never takes effect*
> *while the one who made it is living.... In fact, **the law***
> ***requires that nearly everything be cleansed with***
> ***blood,** and without the shedding of blood there is no*
> *forgiveness.* (Hebrews 9:16, 22 NIV)

A covenant with God didn't go into effect without
blood—and, in fact, death. Even to inaugurate the old covenant, Moses took animal blood and sprinkled it over the
scroll and over the people. (Now, that's a church service we're

willing to miss!) Likewise, the new covenant didn't start until blood was shed—the blood of Jesus on the cross.

This is a revolutionary concept. Most of us grew up believing the New Testament era began with the birth of Jesus. But it didn't. That's not when His blood was shed. Think about it: There was no blood shed for our sins in the manger.

The New Testament era, or the new covenant, began at the *death* of Christ, not His birth. It was Jesus's death on Calvary, not His birth in Bethlehem, that ushered in God's new way of grace. However, when you open most Bibles, there's a big blank page about two-thirds of the way through that says "THE NEW TESTAMENT" in big block letters. Where is that page found? Right before Matthew 1, where the story of Jesus's birth is recorded.

Sure, the page is helpful as it separates the hundreds of years between Malachi and Matthew. But it's *unhelpful* in that the actual New Testament era doesn't begin on any page in a book. It began on a day in human history when the Son of God shed His blood and died.

Without the shedding of blood, there is no forgiveness. And without the death of Jesus, there is no new covenant. We read in Galatians 4:4 that Jesus was born under the Law:

> *But when the fullness of the time came, God sent forth His Son, born of a woman, **born under the Law,** so that He might redeem **those who were under the Law,** that we might receive the adoption as sons.* (Galatians 4:4–5)

Jesus was born into an era of Law-based living. The people around Him were still under the Old Testament way—despite what that divider page in your Bible might say. And it was not until Jesus's death that the new covenant way was brought in. Jesus Himself emphasized this at the Last Supper:

> *This cup which is poured out for you is **the new covenant in My blood**.* (Luke 22:20b)

Each time we take the Lord's Supper, it's a visual reminder of when the new covenant actually began. So understanding the new covenant requires a thirty-three-year shift in our perspective as we move the dividing line of human history from Bethlehem to Calvary.

That's when the new atmosphere of grace really began.

JESUS AMPS IT UP!

Recognizing that Jesus taught people under the old covenant helps us better understand Him. After all, Jesus said some very harsh things at times.

For example, consider his Sermon on the Mount: Cut off your hand. Pluck out your eye. Forgive others to be forgiven. Be perfect like God. He said looking with lust is the same as adultery, and anger is the same as murder. He went on to say both deserve punishment in Hell.

Conversely, He sometimes offered His hearers words of encouragement and good news. He taught them about "abiding in Him" and spoke of how they would one day be indwelt by the Comforter.

Therefore, we have to ask: Why would Jesus teach in two completely different ways? It's hard to understand why if we don't realize Jesus had two goals during His ministry:

1. To show the proud Jews of His day the futility of trying to achieve righteousness under Old Testament law. This is why Jesus offered them impossible standards to live by, including chopping off body parts in their fight against sin (Matthew 5:29–30), selling all their belongings (Luke 18:22), and even being perfect like God (Matthew 5:48).
2. To prophesy to all about a new and better way of grace that would soon arrive through His death and resurrection. For example, this is when He taught about the vine-and-branches relationship with Him and the coming Holy Spirit.

Jesus was frustrating people under the old covenant by showing them how impossible it was for them to get right with God on their own steam. And He was teaching them about the new way to come, in which they could be made perfectly righteous through no effort of their own.

Once we see *both* goals of Jesus, the purpose of His harsh teachings becomes a *lot* clearer. Throughout His ministry, Jesus was offering the hope of God's grace to the humble. But He was also burying proud, religious zealots—who thought they had it all figured out—under the true and impossible standard of the Law. Even this latter motive was one of love because it would ultimately drive the proud to see their need for grace.

NEW COVENANT COMMANDS

The new covenant isn't entirely commandment-free, though. It's just that this time, God's desires are written on our hearts (Hebrews 10:16) instead of stone tablets. What are the new covenant commands etched on the lining of our new-hearted self? *Believe* in Jesus and *love* others even as He loves us:

> *A new commandment I give to you, that you love one another, even as I have loved you, that you also love one another.* (John 13:34)

> *This is His commandment, that we believe in the name of His Son Jesus Christ, and love one another, just as He commanded us.* (1 John 3:23)

It's not the 613 commands of the Old Testament law written on our hearts. No, "believe and love"—these are what our God has written within us with His own hand.

IN WITH THE NEW!

If we don't have the Old Testament law written on our hearts, what is our relationship to it? Throughout the New Testament, God makes it crystal clear:

*But if you are led by the Spirit, **you are not under the Law.*** (Galatians 5:18)

*But now that faith has come, **we are no longer under a tutor [the Law].*** (Galatians 3:25)

*For through the law **I died to the law** so that I might live to God.* (Galatians 2:19)

*But now we have been **released from the Law, having died** to that by which we were bound, so that we serve in newness of the Spirit and not in oldness of the letter.* (Romans 7:6)

***For Christ is the end of the law** for righteousness to everyone who believes.* (Romans 10:4)

God leaves no room for doubt. You're not under the law. You're not under its supervision. You died to it. You've been released from it. And the grand finale: Christ is the end of the law for you because you believe.

It would make no sense for you to have the Old Testament law written inside you. That would be such a message of contradictions:

- You're dead to the Law, but it's on your heart?
- You're not under the Law, but it's on your heart?
- Christ is the end of the Law for you, but it's on your heart?

Not the case! What a liberating message it is that your freedom from the Law is *real* and *absolute*. And this liberty doesn't just relate to salvation. In Galatians 3 and 5, Paul references this freedom in terms of what is *supervising* you and *leading* you on a daily basis.

To see this, just reread the verses on the previous page. Take note of the "so that" expressions and this is what you learn: You died to the Law ...

- so that there may be *righteousness* for you who believe,
- so that you might *live for God*,
- and so that you *serve* in the new way of the Spirit.

Your death to the Law brought righteousness and so much more! Freedom from the Law is what enables you *to live for God* and *serve in the new way of the Spirit*. Dying to the Law is what sets you free in a new and liberating atmosphere of God's grace that inspires you.

Life under the new covenant isn't a life of passivity. Just because you're freed from the Law doesn't mean God intends to sit around—inactive within you—until it's time for you to cash in your ticket to Heaven. No, freedom from the Law actually causes you to bear fruit for God!

*So, my brothers and sisters, **you also died to the law** through the body of Christ, that you might belong to another, to him who was raised from the dead, **in order that we might bear fruit for God**. (Romans 7:4 NIV)*

CHAPTER 16

You may be tracking with us so far concerning this new covenant atmosphere of grace, but we're about to take it a step further. Here it is: Your radical and life-giving freedom from the Law also includes freedom from the Ten Commandments.

That's right—you aren't under the Big Ten. How can we be so sure? Paul makes it clear:

> But if **the ministry of death, in letters engraved on stones,** came with glory, so that the sons of Israel could not look intently at the face of Moses because of the glory of his face, fading as it was, how will the ministry of the Spirit fail to be even more with glory? For if **the ministry of condemnation** has glory, much more does the ministry of righteousness abound in glory. For indeed

what had glory, in this case has no glory because of the glory that surpasses it. For if that which fades away was with glory, much more that which remains is in glory. (2 Corinthians 3:7–11)

These verses are unmistakable. They can't possibly be interpreted to mean ceremonial regulations or dietary restrictions. Paul is specifically talking about a ministry "engraved on stones." And the Ten Commandments were the only part of the Law etched in stone.

So what does Paul say about them? He refers to the Ten Commandments as a "ministry of death" and a "ministry of condemnation." He even goes on to say the Ten Commandments have *no glory* in comparison to the righteousness-giving ministry of the Spirit.

That's pretty incredible. But wait, there's more to drive this point home:

> For I would not have known about coveting if the Law had not said, **"You shall not covet."** But sin, taking opportunity through the commandment, produced in me coveting of every kind; for **apart from the Law sin is dead.** (Romans 7:7b–8)

Here, Paul is again talking about one of the Ten Commandments: "You shall not covet." He says that sin gains an opportunity through the commandment. Then Paul provides the surprising solution: "apart from the Law sin is dead."

Apart from what law? The coveting law—one of the Ten Commandments.

Do you see the radical liberty Paul is speaking of here? If you have a coveting problem, don't trust Moses. Trust Jesus. If you have a stealing problem, don't trust Moses. Trust Jesus. If you have an adultery problem, don't trust Moses. Trust Jesus. He will never lead you to covet or steal or commit adultery. Jesus is enough.

In this same chapter of Romans, Paul says you died to the Law so that you might be joined (married) to Jesus (Romans 7:4). Here's what God is trying to tell you: *Flirting with Moses is cheating on Jesus!*

Under the Ten Commandments, sin is alive. Apart from the Ten Commandments, sin is dead. Yes, it's that simple for a new-hearted person. Have you ever considered that part of the reason you struggle so much with sin is the way you've been fighting it? If you've been trying to fight sin with rule-keeping, no wonder sin seems so alive!

But if you don't look to the Ten Commandments, then what will lead you? The indwelling Christ will inspire you from the heart. Remember that with your new heart comes new commands etched inside: to trust Jesus and love others even as He loves you.

If you're loving someone, you can't steal from them at the same time. If you're loving someone, you can't commit adultery against them at the same time. Apparently, the commands of *believe* and *love* are enough to guide you in so many ways:

*Above all, love each other deeply, because **love covers over a multitude of sins**.* (1 Peter 4:8 NIV)

God is not naïve. He knows exactly how you're designed to work. He knows the genuine solution for your attitudes and actions is not a new set of more detailed or stricter laws. It's exactly the opposite: If you're simply loving others, you won't sin against them.

> **Love does no wrong to a neighbor;** *therefore love is the fulfillment of the law.* (Romans 13:10)

TOTAL RESPECT

This is *not* about disrespecting the Law. No, the Law is holy and righteous and good (Romans 7:12). And Jesus didn't come to abolish the Law but to fulfill it (Matthew 5:17). But because He *did* fulfill it, you don't have to—and you couldn't anyway.

Those who opt for God's grace are the only ones who truly respect the perfect and impossible standard of the Law. Allow us to explain: When people water down the stringency of the Law—cherry-picking just a few of their favorite commands to obey—they give the false impression that the Law only requires they "do their best" and that they'll be graded on a curve. This is disrespectful to the Law! As we'll see, the truth is that the Law only gives two grades—a perfect 100 or a failing 0. And there was only *one* Person who could ever score that perfect 100.

So if we truly respect the Law, we'll recognize it's so perfect and so impossible that we could never meet its standards. This is why rightness with God has to come by grace through faith. Therefore, anyone who flirts with the Law and cherry-picks from it—focusing only on certain commands—is not *really* respecting God's law at all.

NO EXCEPTIONS

Imagine being married to an abusive perfectionist. You can never do it right. They give you a list of twenty things to do over the weekend, and you slave away every hour of the day and get nineteen of them done perfectly. But when you go to check in with your spouse, the only thing they want to talk about is the one thing you failed to do. The next thing you know, they're telling you how you're a sorry, no-good excuse for a spouse.

Similarly, the Law is an all-or-nothing proposition. If you're under the Law, you're under obligation to keep the whole thing—perfectly. You don't get to pick your favorite parts. Both James and Paul make this clear:

> *For whoever keeps the whole law and yet stumbles at just one point **is guilty of breaking all of it.*** (James 2:10 NIV)

> *Mark my words! I, Paul, tell you that if you let yourselves be circumcised, Christ will be of no value to you at all. Again I declare to every man who lets himself be circumcised that he is **obligated to obey the whole law.*** (Galatians 5:2–3 NIV)

> *For all who rely on the works of the law are under a curse, as it is written: **"Cursed is everyone who does not continue to do everything written in the Book of the Law."*** (Galatians 3:10 NIV)

God is not grading on a curve. The Law is simply a "no can do." That's right. Keep six hundred–plus regulations and blow it in only one way, and your score is zero: You're cursed. Notice that it says to continue to do everything written in "the Book of the Law." This refers to the entirety of the Torah with all of its regulations. No exceptions.

SHUT UP!

"Shut up!" That was a forbidden expression in our households growing up. Our mothers just didn't tolerate it. But this is precisely what the Law does with its 613 laws staring us in the face. It shuts us up:

> Now we know that whatever the law says, it says to those who are under the law, **so that every mouth may be silenced** and the whole world held accountable to God. Therefore no one will be declared righteous in His sight by observing the law; rather, **through the law we become conscious of sin.** (Romans 3:19–20 NIV)

Notice the Law has one audience: It's only *unbelievers* who are under it. The Law is designed to silence them, as they have no good response to all its impossible demands. Instead, they only gain a consciousness of sin.

God didn't give the Law to make you alive. He gave the Law to prove you were dead. God didn't give the Law to show you what He's like. He gave the Law to show you what *you* were like.

The giving of the Law was a gracious move in that it served to end the deception of achieved righteousness. The perfect and impossible standard of the Law ultimately leads you to the One who makes you righteous by receiving, not achieving.

This was God's plan from the beginning. When God wanted to show you what He was like, He didn't send the Law. He sent Jesus, Who is the *exact* representation of God the Father (Hebrews 1:3). If your perception of Jesus and your perception of God are different, then they need to be harmonized. Because of Jesus, you don't have to relate to God—through the lens of the Law—as Taskmaster and Judge. You can enjoy Him as your loving Father. So if you want to know what God is like, look to Jesus.

THE PERFECT TUTOR

Here's more evidence that the Law is only speaking to unbelievers:

> *We know that the law is good if one **uses it properly**.*
> *We also know that law is made **not for the righteous**
> *but for lawbreakers and rebels, the ungodly and sinful,*
> *the unholy and irreligious; for those who kill their fathers*
> *or mothers, for murderers, for adulterers and perverts,*
> *for slave traders and liars and perjurers—and for whatever else is contrary to the sound doctrine.* (1 Timothy
> 1:8–10 NIV)

The Law is not made for the righteous (that's you!) but instead for the unbeliever who is still "under the law." The Law in its perfection acts as a schoolmaster, pointing out the world's inability to live up to the standard, keeping it accountable for its shortfall. The Law ultimately reveals spiritual death and addiction to sin:

> *I would not have **come to know sin** except **through the Law**.* (Romans 7:7b)

> *But before faith came, we were kept in custody under the law, being shut up to the faith which was later to be revealed. Therefore **the Law has become our tutor to lead us to Christ**, so that we may be justified by faith.* (Galatians 3:23–24)

Galatians 3 says the Law kept you "in custody" before you had faith in Christ. You were locked up and held prisoner by the Law. Yet we're still hearing a debate today, two thousand years later, about whether the Law should play a role in the Christian life. We're inviting people to prison, and we don't even realize it!

Expect More Struggle, Not Less!

The Law doesn't just *reveal* an addiction to sin. Being under the Law actually *enhances* the addiction!

> *For while we were in the flesh, **the sinful passions,** which were **aroused by the Law**, were at work in the members of our body to bear fruit for death.* (Romans 7:5)

> *For **sin shall not be master over you,** for **you are not under law** but under grace.* (Romans 6:14)

Romans 7 says sinful passions are *aroused* by the Law. Romans 6 reveals that sin masters you under the Law. It's only *apart* from the Law that sin is truly dead (Romans 7:8).

> *The sting of death is sin, and **the power of sin is the law.*** (1 Corinthians 15:56)

Again, if you've ever wondered why you struggle with sin so much, consider the possibility that it's the way you've gone about the battle. If you're fighting sin with a bunch of "thou shalt not" rules, you can expect *more* struggle, not less.

GO WHOLE HOG!

Eight-track cassettes. Phone booths. Movie rental stores. What do they all have in common? They all were once vital but have now become obsolete and disappeared. Did you know the author of Hebrews wrote the same thing about the old covenant? He called the old covenant "obsolete" (Hebrews 8:13). He said the Law is "weak" and "useless" and the new covenant is your better hope (Hebrews 7:18–19).

If you live in the South like us, you're familiar with the two-hundred-year-old expression "Go whole hog!" That's essentially God's message to us in the new covenant: Go whole hog. Or, to put it another way with an even more familiar expression: "Out with the old. In with the new."

Interestingly, *the lineage of Jesus* communicates this best. When we take a look, we discover something that is, at first, alarming. It turns out that Jesus is unqualified to serve as a high priest according to the Law. What? That's right: Jesus was not born into the tribe of Levi and was therefore disqualified to serve as a priest under the Law.

But don't worry, there's a good reason for this! The author of Hebrews explains:

> *For when the priesthood is changed, the law must be changed also.* He of whom these things are said belonged to a different tribe, and no one from that tribe has ever served at the altar. For it is clear that **our Lord descended from Judah, and in regard to that tribe Moses said nothing about priests.** (Hebrews 7:12–14 NIV)

Why not have Jesus be born as the next in a long line of Levitical priests? God did it on purpose: "When the priesthood is changed, the law must be changed also."

You can't take on a little bit of Moses and a little bit of Jesus. You now call upon Jesus from the tribe of Judah, someone who has no business calling himself a priest under the Law. He's from the wrong tribe and therefore ineligible. Yet you're calling him your High Priest. So if you're recognizing a change in priesthood, you must be consistent and likewise recognize *a change in the law.*

Here's God's message to you through the lineage of Jesus: Go whole hog. Be consistent. Recognize Jesus as High Priest *and* recognize the new covenant as your only way forward!

CHAPTER 17

One of the great benefits of living under the new covenant is how secure you are in Jesus. What exactly secures you so firmly? Curiously, it's a promise between God and God. Yes, God promised Himself that you would be safe in Him forever:

> *People swear by someone greater than themselves, and the oath confirms what is said and **puts an end to all argument.** Because God wanted to make the unchanging nature of his purpose very clear to the heirs of what was promised, he confirmed it with an oath. God did this so that, **by two unchangeable things in which it is impossible for God to lie,** we who have fled to take hold of the hope set before us may be greatly*

encouraged. ***We have this hope as an anchor for the
soul, firm and secure.*** (Hebrews 6:16–19a NIV)

The promise is rock solid on both sides. Why? Because
on one side, we see God in all of His faithfulness and consistency and trustworthiness. On the other side, we likewise see
God in all of His faithfulness and consistency and
trustworthiness.

No, you didn't misread that. It's the same God on both
sides of the promise. In contrast, consider the reading of the
Law in Exodus 24 and what that agreement looked like:

> *Then he took the Book of the Covenant and read it to
> the people. They responded,* ***"We will do everything*** *the
> Lord has said; we will obey."* (Exodus 24:7 NIV)

Moses read the Law to the people of Israel. They in turn
promised to do "everything" the Lord had commanded. But
if you remember your history, their promise didn't last long.
No, the Old Testament is filled with stories of failed promise
after failed promise as Israel continually disobeyed God.
That's the problem with any covenant where we humans have
to keep up our end of a bargain. We are destined to fail.

So you can see why God decided to swear by Himself in the
new covenant. He made an agreement with Himself so there'd
be a truth-telling God on one side and a truth-telling God on
the other. He Himself is the anchor for your soul. In this way,
God put an end to every argument about your eternal security.
You're saved and sustained by His promise-keeping, *not* yours.

You're Saved Forever

"But what if I …?" This is how nearly every argument concerning loss of salvation begins. *But what if I commit a ton of sins? But what if I commit the same sin over and over? But what if I commit a sin willfully?* By the way, *every* sin you've ever committed involved your will! Here are two better questions to ask: *But what if it's not about you? But what if Jesus…?*

In this vein, Hebrews 7 says you are saved completely and forever because of Jesus, not you:

> *But because Jesus lives forever, he has a permanent priesthood. Therefore **he is able to save completely** those who come to God through him, **because he always lives** to intercede for them.* (Hebrews 7:24–25 NIV)

How long will you be saved? Forever. Why? Because Jesus lives forever. So you will be saved as long as Jesus lives. Now that's something to celebrate!

You can know for certain that you have eternal life (1 John 5:13). Jesus will never lose you (John 6:39). No one can take you from God's hand (John 10:28–29). And God will never abandon you for any reason (Hebrews 13:5). All of this is true because of God's promise to Himself to save you completely and forever.

A Confident Rest

At salvation, you were invited to rest in all that God accomplished for you:

There remains, then, a Sabbath-rest for the people of God;
for anyone who enters God's rest also rests from his own
work, just as God did from His. Let us, therefore, make
every effort to enter that rest. (Hebrews 4:9–11 NIV)

How do you "make every effort to enter that rest"? As a
believer, you have *already* entered God's rest. You're in the
"promised land" of knowing Jesus Christ and are no longer
in a spiritual wilderness.

But two thousand years ago, the Hebrews needed to make
up their minds about Jesus. If they decided He was the Lamb
of God who takes away their sins and the Son of God who is
eternal life, they could call upon His name to be saved. Then,
they could leave behind Law-based living once and for all and
begin enjoying the new covenant way of "easy" and "light"
(Matthew 11:28–30).

It's clear, then, that one great benefit of living under the new
covenant is that we get *to rest* in a relationship with God that is
not burdensome. But there's another mark of a person who's truly
enjoying God's new covenant way of grace: confidence. Hebrews
10 says you can have confidence in this new and living way
because you can draw near to God with absolute assurance that
you're forgiven and cleansed forever (Hebrew 10:14, 19–23).

The rest and confidence the new covenant brings are awe-
some, but they're only fully enjoyed as we stand firm in the sufficiency of all that Jesus has done.

*It is for **freedom** that Christ has set us free. **Stand firm,***
then, and do not let yourselves be burdened again by a yoke
of slavery. (Galatians 5:1 NIV)

TOO MUCH VICTORY?

Real freedom is not freedom *to* sin. Real freedom is freedom *from* sin.

That's the radical and powerful liberty you enjoy in this new covenant atmosphere of grace. So if you've ever thought that too much grace is dangerous, here's a clear invitation to rethink that premise:

> *For sin shall **not** be master over you, for you are not under law but **under grace**.* (Romans 6:14)

Saying you can have too much grace is like saying you can have too much victory over sin. Can you have too much Law? Yes, the Law arouses sinful passions. You should have no spiritual relationship with the Law now that you have Jesus. But can you have too much grace? No way! You can never have too much freedom from sin's power, and that's what God's grace provides.

THE RULING ON RELIGIOUS RULES

"Okay, okay, I get it. I'm not under the Law. But in order to avoid sin, I still need to live by good Christian principles and rules, right?"

Thou shalt go to church. Thou shalt share your faith. Thou shalt read your Bible. Thou shalt volunteer for the nursery. Thou shalt always say "yes" when asked.

If we're not careful, we end up inventing our own flavor of religious law filled with people-pleasing rules and self-imposed obligations. And as long as we comply with these things, we give ourselves a good score and allow ourselves to feel "closer" to God. But two thousand years ago, Paul warned against this:

> **Since you died with Christ** to the elemental spiritual forces of this world, **why,** as though you still belonged to the world, **do you submit to its rules:** "Do not handle! Do not taste! Do not touch!"? These rules, which have to do with things that are all destined to perish with use, are based on merely human commands and teachings. Such regulations indeed **have an appearance of wisdom,** with their self-imposed worship, their false humility and their harsh treatment of the body, but they **lack any value** in restraining sensual indulgence. (Colossians 2:20–23 NIV)

Rules can seem so religious and feel so right. But give them time, and you'll see they just don't work. Why won't rules work for you? Rules are for dirty people, and you're clean. Rules are for sinful people, and you're a saint. Rules are for sin addicts, and you're a slave of righteousness (Romans 6:18). God designed the new-hearted and perfect you to be inspired in an atmosphere of grace.

So don't look to rules. Let Christ rule.

> **Let the peace of Christ rule in your hearts,** to which indeed you were called in one body; and be thankful. (Colossians 3:15)

THE TREE OF MORALITY AND ETHICS

Chasing after our own system of rule-keeping, morality, and ethics began as early as the Garden of Eden. Remember the tree they ate from? It wasn't "the evil tree." No, it was the tree of the knowledge of *good* and evil.

They were looking to know good from evil, so they could do good and avoid evil. In so doing, they imagined they would become more "godly." After all, that was the sales pitch in the garden:

> *For God knows that in the day you eat from it your eyes will be opened, **and you will be like God, knowing good and evil.*** (Genesis 3:5)

Yes, the carrot on the end of the stick was "godliness." As soon as the first humans were suckered by the sales pitch, they began to measure themselves by a rule or standard. And the inevitable result was *shame*.

God's response: "Who told you that you were naked?" (Genesis 3:11).

Keep in mind that they'd lived life naked since the day they were created by God. But suddenly, there was a system of measuring in place. They'd eaten from the tree of morality and ethics, and now they deemed themselves unworthy and in need of covering.

They had believed the lie that God was holding out on them. The truth is that He was protecting them from the total disaster of abandoning the dependent life and choosing "religion" instead. An achieving system had replaced the receiving system. The way of "good" had replaced the way of grace. Religious measuring was a death trap then, and it is today.

A Grace Atmosphere

Given the boundless freedom we enjoy, we must ask: What is our source? What motivates everything that we say or do? Is it merely a set of religious principles, or are we guided by our new hearts where Christ dwells?

> *Neither circumcision nor uncircumcision means anything; **what counts is the new creation.** Peace and mercy to all who **follow this rule**—to the Israel of God.* (Galatians 6:15–16 NIV)

Here, Paul mentions a rule, but not one in the traditional sense. No, it's the rule of the new creation: Knowing who you are in Christ and being yourself. This is what counts! The new-hearted, perfect you doesn't need a set of laws to govern your behavior. You can let God's grace rule!

> *For **the grace of God** that brings salvation has appeared to all men. **It teaches us to say "No" to ungodliness and worldly passions, and to live self-controlled, upright and godly lives** in this present age, while we wait for the blessed hope—the glorious appearing of our great God and Savior, Jesus Christ, who gave Himself for us to redeem us from all wickedness and to purify for*

*Himself a people that are His very own, eager to do
what is good.* (Titus 2:11–14 NIV)

By God's grace, you've been transformed into the new-
hearted, perfect you who is *eager* to bear fruit. And God's
atmosphere of grace is your motivator. Grace is way more than
forgiveness when you fail. God's grace inspires you to live an
upright life.

The importance of preserving this atmosphere is why the
Apostle Paul called the Galatians "foolish." He was frustrated
that they were so quickly abandoning grace for an alternative
atmosphere of fleshly perfectionism:

> *You foolish Galatians, who has bewitched you,
> before whose eyes Jesus Christ was publicly portrayed
> as crucified? This is the only thing I want to find
> out from you:* **did you receive the Spirit by the
> works of the Law, or by hearing with faith? Are
> you so foolish? Having begun by the Spirit, are
> you now being perfected by the flesh?** *Did you
> suffer so many things in vain—if indeed it was in
> vain?* (Galatians 3:1–4)

Paul offers them multiple choice. He first asks them how
they were saved—by the Law or by faith? Second, he asks
them how they plan to grow—by the Law or by faith?

Paul was appalled that they'd answer one way for salvation
and another way for growth. It's supposed to be God's grace
from start to finish!

*So then, **just as you received** Christ Jesus as Lord, **continue** to live your lives in him.* (Colossians 2:6 NIV)

PART 7

THE PERFECT SACRIFICE

CHAPTER 18

An atmosphere of grace is essential to the perfect you. But there's more to it than just being freed from the Law and knowing God's full acceptance.

You've committed so many sins in your lifetime and so many since you became a believer. So it's easy to be suckered by the sales pitch of self-improvement when your many sins are being flashed before your eyes every day by the Accuser. How distracting, to say the least!

What is God's solution? The perfect sacrifice.

God doesn't bring you just any sort of forgiveness. As we'll see, God has provided you with what He calls "once for all" forgiveness. This radical flavor of forgiveness is unlike anything you've experienced before, and it miraculously enables you to stay focused on the perfect you in union with Jesus.

An Atmosphere of Forgiveness

Forgiveness is actually a very controversial topic for Christians. The simple message that you're totally forgiven for your sins—past, present, and future (even the sins you haven't committed yet)—can make many people angry. (But don't worry—they're forgiven for getting angry too!)

"Does sin not matter?" they ask. And of course, our behavior absolutely matters. But you know what? Christians were asking the Apostle Paul this same question two thousand years ago after he explained God's grace to them. When people heard Paul's message of limitless grace in Jesus Christ, this was often their response: "Are we to continue in sin so that grace may increase?" (Romans 6:1).

Logically, this question should come up. It has to come up! After all, if this question of "Why not just sin?" does not arise, then something is wrong with the message we're believing.

The Gospel—with its "once-for-all" forgiveness—begs this question.

And here's the answer: You've died to sin. You're the new-hearted self. You're a slave of righteousness. You hate sin and love Jesus. You can't help it. God's not naïve. You can afford to be this forgiven. Paul expresses it this way: "How shall we who died to sin still live in it?" (Romans 6:2b).

So now that we've clarified the importance of good behavior and fruit-bearing, can we talk about just how amazing this once-for-all forgiveness from Jesus really is?

Here we go!

Once-for-All Forgiveness

Under the Old Testament law, forgiveness was issued in "installments," like paying off your mortgage or your car. Once each year at the Day of Atonement, the Jews would offer sacrifices for their sins. The blood of that sacrifice would cover—not take away, but cover—their sins of the past year.

But if they stubbed their toe and cursed on the way home from the Day of Atonement, they'd be right back where they started with a spotted sin record. They'd have to go back next year—and every year—for more forgiveness and more cleansing. This is what the Bible calls "again and again" forgiveness (Hebrews 10:11), the opposite of the once-for-all forgiveness we enjoy today (Hebrews 10:12, 14).

The Law could never, by the same sacrifices repeated endlessly, year after year, make perfect those who drew near to worship. If any one of those sacrifices had been perfect, they could've stopped offering them!

> *Otherwise, would they not have ceased to be offered,*
> *because the worshipers, **having once been cleansed,***
> *would no longer have had consciousness of sins?*
> (Hebrews 10:2)

Do you see it? If one of those sacrifices had been remotely comparable to the finished work of Jesus Christ, those worshippers would've been cleansed once for all and freed from a guilty conscience forever.

Now let's put *you* in the picture. Here you are, living on *this* side of the cross, under the new covenant. The sacrifice for your sins was not an animal; it was the perfect Lamb of God. Therefore, you have a flavor of forgiveness that those in the Old Testament never enjoyed.

You're *not* being forgiven progressively in installments. Because of Jesus's "once-for-all" sacrifice on the cross, you're totally forgiven and cleansed of all sins—past, present, and future.

> For Christ died for sins **once for all,** the righteous for the unrighteous, to bring you to God. (1 Peter 3:18a)

> For **by one offering He has perfected for all time** those who are sanctified. (Hebrews 10:14)

He Sat Down!

Under the old covenant, the sacrifices were never finished. No, the Levitical priests were always standing, constantly offering more sacrifices. Their work was never done. It was never "finished." And that's the whole point!

In contrast, after serving as the sacrifice for our sins, our High Priest, Jesus Christ, did what no other priest before Him could ever do. He sat down:

> But He, having offered one sacrifice for sins for all time, **sat down** at the right hand of God, waiting from that time onward until His enemies be made a footstool for His feet. **For by one offering He has perfected for all time those who are sanctified.** (Hebrews 10:12–14)

*When He had made purification of sins, **He sat
down** at the right hand of the Majesty on high.*
(Hebrews 1:3b)

What does this mean for you that Jesus sat down? It
means He'll never do anything more to deal with your
sin record. It's over. It's done. Your sins will never be
taken into account. They're gone forever (Romans 4:8).
Jesus is resting in a reclined position concerning your sins.
Why? Because you've been "made perfect forever"
(Hebrews 10:14).

The question for you is this: What position are *you* in
about your sins? Are you standing up like those Old Testament priests, trying to get more and more forgiveness and
cleansing? Or are you sitting down with Jesus, agreeing
with Him that the sin issue between you and God is over?

In other words, are you suffering from "the Martha
Syndrome"—standing up, even frantically running around
like Martha was in the kitchen as she sought to get everything clean and right for Jesus? Or are you acting more like
Mary—seated with Jesus, relaxed, and enjoying Him?

Given what Jesus has done to forgive you—once for
all—which do you think is a response of faith?

THE GREAT TAKEAWAY

Christ did not die to "cover" a year of your sins like the
old covenant sacrifices did at the Day of Atonement. No,
the cross of Christ brought a total takeaway of your sins:

> *But those sacrifices are an annual reminder of sins,
> because it is impossible for the blood of bulls and goats to
> **take away** sins.* (Hebrews 10:4 NIV)

> *The next day John saw Jesus coming toward him and
> said, "Look, the Lamb of God, who **takes away** the sin
> of the world!"* (John 1:29)

> *But you know that He appeared so that He might **take
> away** our sins. And in Him is no sin.* (1 John 3:5 NIV)

This means your sins have been removed forever. Because Christ offered a perfect sacrifice for your sins, He could truly say, "It is finished."

Now, if you've spent any time in the book of Hebrews, maybe you've noticed that the writer will not let his readers say "Amen" to Christ's finished work and then five minutes later believe they need more forgiveness. Nope. No double-talk allowed: Christ died once. It worked the first time. No repeat needed. And that means no more forgiveness is needed either!

The Jewish believers of that day were very conscious of something we don't think or talk about much today—God's "blood economy" for forgiveness of sins:

> *And according to the Law, one may almost say, all things
> are cleansed with blood, and **without shedding of blood
> there is no forgiveness.*** (Hebrews 9:22)

So, they could connect the dots easily: Only blood brings forgiveness. Jesus shed his blood once. He's *not* up in Heaven shedding more blood, over and over. Therefore, we're as forgiven today as we'll ever be!

That's the powerful message found at the center of the epistle to the Hebrews. Unfortunately, Hebrews is one of the least studied letters in the Church these days. As a result, many believers today are unsure of exactly how forgiven they really are.

PAST, BUT NOT FUTURE SINS?

In fact, here's a very common belief today: "We're forgiven of our past sins but *not* our future sins. We're only forgiven of the sins we confess to God." (Some even think they lose their salvation every time they sin until they properly repent and ask for forgiveness.)

Without even realizing it, you can end up buying into a belief system that plays out like this:

You're forgiven of all your sins, unless you sin. Jesus took away all your sins and remembers your sins no more, except if you commit one. Then it's up to you to get more forgiveness. So make sure you don't accidentally forget to confess one.

We end up mixing our New Testament High Priest— Jesus—with an Old Testament concept of progressive forgiveness. In this way, we belittle the finished work of Jesus Christ. Hebrews makes it clear that Christ is not up in Heaven dying over and over. This means we're not down here on Earth being forgiven over and over. It really is finished:

> *For Christ did not enter a man-made sanctuary that was only a copy of the true one; He entered heaven itself,*

*now to appear for us in God's presence, **nor did He enter
heaven to offer Himself again and again,** the way the
high priest enters the Most Holy Place every year with
blood that is not his own. Then Christ would have had
to **suffer many times** since the creation of the world. But
now He has appeared **once for all** at the end of the ages
to do away with sin by the sacrifice of Himself.*
(Hebrews 9:25–26 NIV)

It's No Better Today

When a Hebrew read this two thousand years ago, it came
across as pretty radical. This was essentially the message:
*There's no sacrifice left for sins. Don't go back to the Temple and
expect anything new to happen. Don't put another animal on the
altar. It's purposeless now. God has closed up shop on your forgiveness. It's over. Jesus did it all on the Cross. He did it perfectly and
completely the first time. No redo needed.*

Now our guess is that you're probably not sacrificing animals for your sins in your backyard. But when you think that
it's about you and your apologies and your many words, it's
just as bad as the Jews thinking it was about the dead works
of the Temple. If you think it's about keeping short accounts
and getting forgiven progressively each day, you might as well
be a Hebrew from thousands of years ago going to the Temple
despite the message of Christ.

*Then he adds: "Their sins and lawless acts I will remem-
ber no more." And where these have been forgiven,*

sacrifice for sin is no longer necessary. (Hebrews
10:17–18 NIV)

Consider this: No one is 62 percent forgiven. You're either
0 percent forgiven in Adam or 100 percent forgiven in Christ.
There is no in-between. God has not partially forgiven
anyone!

And consider this: How many of your sins were in the
future when Christ died? All of them—the sins before salvation and the sins after salvation were all in the future when
Christ died. That's why *all* your sins are forgiven—past, present, and future. The time of occurrence is irrelevant.

The Law introduced a blood-based system for forgiveness
of sins. Through Christ's one-time blood sacrifice, all our sins
were taken away—once. So either we agree with this statement or we don't:

Because of Jesus, I am 100 percent forgiven no matter what.

And if we don't agree with it, we're saying something else
needs to be done. But don't be deceived. There's nothing else
to be done. If you're in Jesus Christ, your sins have been taken
away once for all. You've been perfectly forgiven forever (John
1:29; Hebrews 10:2, 14).

It's in this atmosphere of total forgiveness that God inspires
you to keep your eyes off your sins and on your Savior!

CHAPTER 19

As clear as the message of "once-for-all" forgiveness is, we often hear popular Bible teachers say something different: "Sure, total forgiveness is true in God's heavenly bookkeeping. But here on Earth, you've got to keep short accounts with God. You still need *experiential* forgiveness, and it's up to you to make it happen."

But see, that's more like Judaism than Christianity. Under the old covenant of Judaism, it *was* up to you. You had to go back once a year to the Day of Atonement to get more forgiveness. And what you often hear in Christian circles today is actually *much worse* than old-covenant forgiveness!

How is it worse? At least under Judaism, the process of getting your sins covered occurred once a year. The blood of animals covered an entire year's worth of sins. And once they were covered, you didn't have to return for a full year.

So what are we saying when we Christians believe we need to get forgiven four times a day, ten times a week, or once every church service? We're saying the blood of Christ is *even less powerful* than the blood of bulls and goats!

With a bit of mental gymnastics, we end up with a theology that's essentially double-talk: We're totally forgiven "positionally," but we still need to get forgiven "relationally." Then we haul out our daily system for more forgiveness and cleansing.

All the while, it's an insult to the blood of Jesus Christ. Remember that Jews felt real-world relief after the animal sacrifices. They felt forgiven positionally, relationally, experientially, and in every way. They didn't have categories for "heavenly bookkeeping" versus "earthly bookkeeping." They just knew their sins were covered, period. How much more can we "feel better" once for all because of the one-time sacrifice of Jesus Christ?

YOU DON'T OWE GOD!

When you owe somebody money and you're hanging out with them, you might feel a little uncomfortable, maybe even awkward. Eventually, you know you're supposed to pay up.

Now, imagine if you owe *the God of the universe!*

You'll hear this sort of thing in some churches on Sunday morning: "Given how much He's done for you ... (long pause for you to feel guilty), how much more should you live to pay Him back?" Then that sense of obligation and guilt sets in. You know whatever you do will never be enough. So you either give it everything you've got, or you resign yourself to feeling a constant sense of guilt from unpaid debt.

But you also may know what it's like when you're released from a debt. You breathe that huge sigh of relief. Well, here's a newsflash: You don't owe God. You don't have to walk on eggshells with Him.

> *He made you alive together with Him,* **having forgiven us all our transgressions, having canceled out the certificate of debt** *consisting of decrees against us.* (Colossians 2:13a–14b)

God forgave you of all your sins. He canceled all your debt. You don't have to lie awake at night wondering what God thinks of you. You don't owe Him a thing. You could never pay Him back anyway.

This directly contradicts a whole lot of fiery preaching out there concerning what you supposedly owe God. Sermons like that make you feel terrible inside, and some interpret that as, "Wow, the Spirit was really convicting me!" Yes, some people actually measure the effectiveness of a sermon by how guilty they feel when it's over. If they feel awful, then God was really moving, and it was a great sermon.

But God already moved in canceling your debt, so guilt is not from Him. God leads you toward freedom, not guilt. He leads you toward an awareness that you're clean and close and debt-free before Him. He never leads you to a sense that you need to pay Him back, as if you could.

Bragging on Jesus

When some people first come to understand the incredible message of "once-for-all" forgiveness, they don't know how to communicate it well. They put the focus solely on what they don't have to do, saying things like, "I don't have to ask for forgiveness for my sins. I'm totally forgiven forever!" Then they walk away with no further explanation. They're going for a shock effect.

If you approach it like that—emphasizing what you *don't* have to do—people will likely misunderstand you to mean that sin doesn't matter and that behavior in general is unimportant to you. It's not actually what you're saying, but they *will* interpret you that way.

We've found that the right focus is to brag on what Jesus did rather than on what you don't have to do. Bragging on Jesus is never a bad thing, and it puts the spotlight on the Cross and what it accomplished in comparison with Old Testament sacrifices.

Notice how the Apostle John expresses his thoughts:

> *I write to you, dear children, because **your sins have been forgiven on account of His name.*** (1 John 2:12 NIV)

First, your sins have been forgiven—past tense! It's not happening. It has happened. But notice why it has happened—*on account of His name*. Why did God do this? To show off the name of Jesus. This incredible forgiveness you possess is not ultimately about you. It's about bragging on the name of Jesus. You're simply a beneficiary of His finished work.

PASSING IT ON

Your belief systems are going to show, whether you realize it or not. You're going to transmit to others whatever treatment you think you're getting from God. So what kind of treatment do you believe you're getting? What kind of grace? What kind of forgiveness?

Once you learn about God's total forgiveness of your sins, you can begin reflecting that type of forgiveness toward those around you:

> *Be kind and compassionate to one another, **forgiving each other, just as in Christ God forgave you**.* (Ephesians 4:32 NIV)

God forgave you completely, so pass it on. But can you see that if you think it's up to you to get forgiven and stay forgiven by God, then you're going to pass on *that* kind of forgiveness to others?

"I'll forgive her after she comes over here and apologizes."

You'll mirror what you *believe* is coming from God. So what if you realize God has given you a total and unconditional release from all your sins and that He's not waiting for apologies? This too would affect the way you'd treat others. You wouldn't wait for a recognition of wrong. You could choose to forgive them and cancel their debt right away—with no strings attached—just as God did for you.

WHAT ABOUT THE LORD'S PRAYER?

Okay, but doesn't the Lord's Prayer say your forgiveness is conditional, based on how you forgive others?

> *And **forgive us** our debts, **as we also have forgiven** our debtors.* (Matthew 6:12)

> *For **if** you forgive others for their transgressions, your heavenly Father **will** also forgive you. But **if** you do not forgive others, then your Father **will not** forgive your transgressions.* (Matthew 6:14–15)

Notice the condition. First, Jesus models a prayer for them in which they should ask God to forgive them just like they've forgiven other people. Ouch. That's going to turn out badly! Second, Jesus reaffirms His meaning by clearly laying out the conditions: If you forgive others, God will forgive you. If you don't forgive others, God will not forgive you.

How does this fit with your once-for-all forgiveness in Christ? After all, how can you be totally forgiven forever but then only be forgiven if you forgive others first? Seems like a contradiction.

Well, it *is* a contradiction!

Remember that Jesus was "born under the Law," and He taught an audience that was still "under the Law" (Galatians 4:4–5). It wasn't until the cross that God's new covenant way of grace began (Hebrews 9:17). This is why so often we find Jesus exposing the fallacy of self-righteousness and the true spirit of the Law: *Cut off your hand. Pluck out your eye. Be perfect like God. Sell everything you own.* This is simply more of the same: *Forgive others to be forgiven by God.*

Jesus was pushing the Jews of His day to realize what they deserve under a Law-based system. And He does the same thing in the next chapter:

> *Do not judge so that you will not be judged.* ***For in the way you judge, you will be judged;*** *and by your standard of measure, it will be measured to you.* (Matthew 7:1–2)

Should Christians worry we'll only be forgiven if we forgive other people first? Should we worry we'll be judged by the same standard employed when we were critical of others? No, of course not! You're forgiven because of the blood of Jesus, not because you were nice to other people. And you can be free from the fear of judgment, since there's no condemnation for those who are in Christ (Romans 8:1).

The Lord's Prayer and its theology of forgiveness only make sense when you recognize that Jesus was teaching before the cross, before His blood was shed for our sins. His audience was a group of Jews who were still living under the Law. And His goal was to expose them to the true spirit of the Law—a perfect and impossible standard—so they'd see their need for God's grace offered through the cross and His resurrection.

So how is forgiving other people taught—after the cross—to New Testament believers?

Bear with each other and forgive one another if any of you has a grievance against someone. **Forgive** *as the Lord* **forgave** *you.* (Colossians 3:13 NIV)

Be kind to one another, tender-hearted, **forgiving** *each other, just as God in Christ also* **has forgiven** *you.* (Ephesians 4:32)

This is the polar opposite of what we see in Matthew 6. Here, Paul is saying to forgive others because God *already* forgave you. There isn't a condition for you to be forgiven—it is finished. You're simply called to share the grace you've *already* received.

"WHAT DO I DO?"

Maybe you're at the point of saying: "Okay, I get it. Forgiveness is based on blood, and Jesus will never shed His blood again. It worked the first time. No repeat needed. So I'm totally forgiven of all my sins—past, present, and future. It really is finished. I get that. But if I don't have to ask God to swoop down out of Heaven to forgive me and cleanse me more each time I sin, then what's a healthy response after sinning?"

We're so used to begging, pleading, even groveling, that perhaps we've missed the obvious: Thank God for our forgiveness. Turn from it. Act differently. Get away from temptation. All of this is a no-brainer!

There's no question that sin is unhealthy. Remember: You're the new-hearted self, the perfect you. You're dead to sin. You're not made for it anymore. It never truly fulfills you.

It's only sensible that you turn from sin and choose to get away from it.

But no amount of stopping and no amount of getting away from it makes you more forgiven. *Turning from sin makes you more fulfilled but not more forgiven.* Yes, a Christian can be totally forgiven yet miserable. So you don't turn from sin to get more forgiven. You turn from sin to once again find true contentment in acting like the new-hearted, perfect you!

CHAPTER 20

O nce you understand that you're totally forgiven, other questions surface:

Why confess your sins? What's the point?

In the Greek, *homologeo* ("confess") means saying the same thing as someone else or agreeing with them. Confession is simply agreeing with God. Is it healthy for you to agree with God? Of course!

You should agree with God about everything.

You confess (agree with God) that Jesus Christ died for your sins. You confess (agree with God) that by His sacrifice you're forgiven. You can also confess (agree with God) that even though you commit sins, you're still righteous. Yes, you can agree with God about the many truths found in the Gospel message.

But as a believer, confessing your sins doesn't make Jesus hang on a cross again. And confessing your sins doesn't make you more forgiven than you already are. No matter how many times you confess your struggles, you remain at the same level of forgiveness the whole time—100 percent forgiven because of Christ's blood, not your confessions.

CONFESSION TO OTHERS

What about confession of sins to one another? Doesn't the Bible say it's important?

> *Therefore, **confess your sins to one another, and pray for one another** so that you may be healed. The effective prayer of a righteous man can accomplish much.* (James 5:16)

It's healthy for you to admit your wrongdoing and to share your struggles with trusted friends in a safe community. So that you can be more forgiven by God? No! You're *already* forgiven. James is saying to share your struggles with others *so they can pray for you.*

Otherwise, how can you pray for a friend and they pray for you unless you both know what's happening in each other's lives? But your confiding in a friend (or not) doesn't affect the completeness of Christ's work.

So again, there are many reasons to admit wrongdoing and confess your struggles, but getting more forgiveness from God is not one of those reasons. It is finished!

THE GREAT DILEMMA

We've already looked at the Lord's Prayer and how Jesus was speaking to people before the cross, before the option of total forgiveness was available to them. But there's another passage written by the Apostle John *after* the cross. It's often misinterpreted and used as fuel for the "You're not forgiven unless you confess each individual sin" theology. Here it is:

> ***If we confess our sins,*** *He is faithful and righteous to forgive us our sins and to cleanse us from all unrighteousness.* (1 John 1:9)

If we confess our sins? What if we don't confess each one? What if we forget one? What if we leave a few out of our confession ritual? Are we then not forgiven by God? Unfortunately, a lot of people believe that! And 1 John 1:9 is the catalyst for their belief.

But is John really saying you should keep a running tally of every sin you commit and be certain to verbally confess each one to God? And must you do this in order to keep a clean slate with God? Of course not. That would go against everything you see throughout the New Testament concerning your "once for all" forgiveness.

Therefore, understanding this verse in context is absolutely critical to being confident about your total forgiveness. A large portion of John's epistle serves to contrast believers and deceivers. As we'll see, this is exactly what is happening in his first chapter.

"If We Confess …"

First, let's be clear: This passage *definitely* carries a clear and conditional *if*: "If we confess …" Furthermore, the (subjunctive) verb phrase that follows indicates doubt about whether a person will or will not confess and thereby be forgiven and cleansed. In other words, the condition *must* be met for them to be forgiven. If they confess, they will be cleansed. If they do not confess, they will not be cleansed. This is what 1 John 1:9 is saying, plain and simple.

If you are a born-again believer, though, as we've already seen, you're totally forgiven and cleansed for all time (Hebrews 10:14). And that's because of the blood of Christ, not because you're able to tally and confess each sin. So how do we properly understand 1 John 1:9?

Often, we assume every verse in the Bible is written to and about Christians. But not so fast! Don't forget the Apostle John's evangelistic heart. Notice that John wanted them to have fellowship with God like he already enjoyed:

> *What we have seen and heard we proclaim to you also,*
> **so that you too may have fellowship with us;** *and*
> *indeed our fellowship is with the Father, and with His*
> *Son Jesus Christ.* (1 John 1:3)

Some of the people to whom John was writing obviously didn't have fellowship with God yet. But do *you* already have fellowship with God? If you're a believer, then the answer is *yes*! When did it begin? When you accepted God's free gift of forgiveness and new life. As a life statement you can say:

"My fellowship is with the Father, and with His Son Jesus Christ." Some of John's audience couldn't say that yet. And that's why he was writing to them!

GETTING MORE CONTEXT

Two thousand years ago, when John was writing his letter, an early form of Gnosticism was being spread throughout the church. First, the Gnostics claimed that *Jesus was not physical*, because God would never stoop so low as to take on a human body. Second, the Gnostics claimed that *sin was not real or didn't matter*. Now, watch as John addresses the first of these heresies at the opening of his letter:

> *What was from the beginning, what we have **heard**, what we have **seen** with our eyes, what we have **looked at** and **touched** with our hands, concerning the Word of Life—and the life was manifested, and we have **seen** and testify and proclaim to you the eternal life, which was with the Father and was **manifested** to us—what we have **seen** and **heard** we proclaim to you also.…* (1 John 1:1–3a)

John was emphasizing the fact that Jesus was indeed physical. John heard, saw, and touched Jesus. In this way, John was combating the first Gnostic heresy. As the chapter continues, he addresses the *second* Gnostic heresy:

> *If we say that we have no sin, we are deceiving ourselves and the truth is not in us. If we confess our sins,*

He is faithful and righteous to forgive us our sins and to cleanse us from all unrighteousness. **If we say that we have not sinned**, *we make Him a liar and His word is not in us.* (1 John 1:8–10)

This Gnostic context reveals the true meaning of 1 John 1:9. John was addressing Gnostic sin deniers in hopes they would come to their senses, admit the truth, and get saved. In so doing, they would be forgiven and cleansed of *all* unrighteousness.

In summary, this is an evangelistic passage written to anyone who says they have no sin (verse 8) and says they've never sinned (verse 10). John goes on to say that those people are deceiving themselves, they are making God a liar, and they don't have the Truth (Jesus) or His Word in them.

Meet Our Friend Joe!

Now, imagine we introduce you to someone: "Here's our friend Joe. Joe says he has never sinned a day in his life. Yeah, Joe says he's sinless. So Joe is calling God a liar, and God's Word has no place in Joe's life."

After hearing us introduce Joe, do you conclude he's a believer? Of course not! Joe can't be a believer because the first step to becoming a believer is admitting you're a sinner in need of a Savior.

Joe isn't ready to do that.

But seeing Joe's stubbornness, you decide to reason with him: "Joe, listen. If you'll just confess your sinfulness to God, then guess what He can do in your life? He will forgive you and cleanse you of all unrighteousness!"

Joes scratches his head a minute in thought and then decides, "You know, you're right. Come to think of it, I have sinned. I am a sinner. I do need forgiveness and cleansing of all unrighteousness. I'm going to take Jesus up on His offer."

This is the true motive behind 1 John 1:9. It's an appeal to Gnostic sin-deniers (or anyone like Joe) to come to their senses, confess their sinfulness, and accept God's once-for-all forgiveness.

By the way, did you notice the word "all" in the verse? Yes, people like Joe can be forgiven and cleansed of "all unrighteousness." No, this verse isn't about getting little-by-little forgiveness with each verbal confession. This is about coming to faith in Christ and by one sacrifice being made perfectly forgiven forever (Hebrews 10:14).

A One-of-a-Kind Verse

With this in mind for 1 John 1:9, do you see that you're reading someone else's mail? Contrary to what many believe, 1 John 1:9 is not a bar of soap for Christians to engage in a daily cleansing ritual.

Think about it: If there were a formula for daily cleansing, then Paul never wrote the Romans about it. The Galatians never heard a word about it. Likewise, the Ephesians and Philippians and Corinthians apparently never got the news. (If anybody needed a formula for keeping short accounts with God, it would've been those Corinthians!)

1 John 1:9 is a one-of-a-kind verse for a reason. It was intended to appeal to sin-deniers, begging them to come to their senses and receive forgiveness and cleansing of *all* unrighteousness—just like we believers already have.

REDEEMED AND FORGIVEN

You don't ask God, "Will You redeem me?" every day, do you? Why not? Because you've already been redeemed. You've been purchased, bought back by God. So, there's no need to ask for redemption over and over.

Here's our point: You were forgiven *at the same time* you were redeemed. It was a two-for-one deal! You didn't get one without the other:

> *In Him we have **redemption** through His blood, **the forgiveness of sins**, in accordance with the riches of God's grace.* (Ephesians 1:7 NIV)

> *For He has rescued us from the dominion of darkness and brought us into the kingdom of the Son He loves, in Whom we have **redemption**, **the forgiveness of sins**.* (Colossians 1:13–14 NIV)

The redemption and the forgiveness came together in Christ. If you're not seeking to get more redeemed each day, why are you seeking to get more forgiven each day? If you've got one, you've got both.

FINALITY THOUGHTS

The finality of the cross means more than redemption and forgiveness. It means you have permanent peace with God. You've been "reconciled."

> *Once you were alienated from God and were enemies in your minds because of your evil behavior. But now **He has reconciled you** by Christ's physical body through death **to present you holy in His sight, without blemish and free from accusation.** (Colossians 1:21–22)*

Holy. Spotless. Blameless. That's the message here. You've been perfectly reconciled to God. You are as clean and close as you can ever get. You have to be! There's no other way to have a permanent relationship and a permanent bond with a perfect God. You had to be made perfectly forgiven, perfectly reconciled, and perfectly righteous. And this is precisely why you don't have to worry about any condemnation or judgment. You're free from both!

> *Therefore **there is now no condemnation for those who are in Christ Jesus.** For the law of the Spirit of life in Christ Jesus has set you free from the law of sin and death. (Romans 8:1–2)*

*For God did not send His Son into the world to judge the world, but to save the world through Him. **Whoever believes in Him is not judged,** but whoever does not believe stands judged already because he has not believed in the name of God's one and only Son.* (John 3:17–18)

It's time to celebrate the finality of the cross which brought you total forgiveness, freedom from all punishment, and absolute peace with God.

*When He had received the drink, Jesus said, **"It is finished."** With that, He bowed His head and gave up His spirit.* (John 19:30 NIV)

The finished work of Christ is the atmosphere God has provided for your new-hearted self to flourish. God's incredible "once-for-all" forgiveness offers you the freedom to learn and grow without the fear of failure. Because you're totally forgiven—past, present, and future—you can take the "risk" of trusting the indwelling Christ with every move you make. And you're free to be the perfect you!

PART 8

THE PERFECT PERSPECTIVE

CHAPTER 21

God's perfect atmosphere for the perfect you is freedom and forgiveness.

There's such beauty in discovering you no longer need to make frantic attempts to get right and stay right with God. You can jettison all the worries that once consumed you: *Am I confessing enough? Praying enough? Reading enough? Serving enough? Being enough?* You start to ease into a healthier outlook. It's no longer about you. It's about Him.

How do you make this happen? Let's put the pieces together from what you've already seen to discover just how you can keep your eyes fixed on Jesus and enjoy your union with Him. We begin with the art of doing nothing. Nothing?

Yes, nothing!

THE ART OF DOING NOTHING

Here's a bit of Italian for starters: *Dolce far niente*. This popular expression means "the sweetness of doing nothing." No, it doesn't refer to being lazy. It simply speaks to the pleasure one gets from being still, from relaxing. Another way to put it is "pleasant relaxation" or "carefree stillness."

Now, doesn't that sound good?

What if you could do that without a flight to Italy or a trip to the beach? What if you could enjoy this "carefree stillness" in the midst of your normal, everyday life?

This is *exactly* what happens when Jesus relieves you of what's been plaguing you: You can then begin to enjoy the absence of that very thing. That is the "sweet nothingness" we're talking about: a lack of concern because what was there is no more.

Sure, there are plenty of important decisions to make when temptation comes knocking, when there's an opportunity to love someone, or when there's any chance to express Jesus. The "art of doing nothing" we're talking about has zero to do with passivity.

It's simply about ditching the religious guilt and all the human effort you've exerted to get God to be pleased with you and to stay on His good side. All of that can come to a screeching halt, because of the finished work of Christ and the perfect you. Ultimately, the art of doing nothing is about refusing to be moved away from the confidence you have in Jesus.

WHAT NOT TO DO

When it comes to what you don't have to do, we want to be clear—this message is for *believers*.

We're talking about the joy and freedom we have *already* in Jesus Christ. (If you're not yet a believer, you can call on the name of the Lord Jesus Christ right now to be saved by His death and resurrection. When you open the door of your life to Him, He promises to come in, transform you, and be with you forever.)

We also want to be clear that, again, there are plenty of things for believers *to* do. As we survey the New Testament, we find dozens of passages describing attitudes and actions. And every day we're faced with plenty of decisions to make: We offer our bodies to God. We walk by the Spirit. We set our minds on truth. We love other people as Jesus loves us.

But here are four things many believers think they have to do:

1. Try to get closer to God.
2. Seek forgiveness and cleansing.
3. Examine or change your heart.
4. Feel or "experience" more.

These four things can consume a lot of your time and energy. They can dominate a lot of your thought processes as you try to relate to God and live the Christian life.

But imagine if you lived every day free of worry about getting closer to God or getting more forgiven. Imagine if you lived every day without trying to "examine" or "change" your heart. Imagine if you didn't have to "feel more spiritual" or chase after an experience of God anymore.

What would your life be like if it were simply marked by *a confident knowing* of the truth?

THE EXAMPLE OF ABRAHAM

A good example of *failing* to practice "the art of doing nothing" would be Abraham. God gave him a promise that he would have a son. God said that through that son, Abraham would be "a father of many nations" (Genesis 17:5).

It was a beautiful promise from the mouth of God Himself, yet what did Abraham do? Abraham did *not* do nothing. Instead, he did something.

Abraham grew nervous when his wife Sarah did not get pregnant on what he perceived to be a reasonable timeline. With a little prodding from Sarah, Abraham decided it was up to him to fulfill God's promise. So he concocted a Plan B with another woman. We all know how that turned out! Even today, thousands of years later, the descendants of that son are locked in endless conflict with the descendants of the promised son from Sarah.

Abraham could have chosen to relax and practice the art of doing nothing. He could have chosen to believe that God was going to make good on His promise. But instead, Abraham went about frantically trying to achieve what God had planned and promised.

Just like Abraham, you might be tempted to try to "help" God. You might be tempted to help Him make you closer, or help Him forgive you, or help Him cleanse your heart, or help Him give you "more" spiritually. And the only thing that'll stop that train is to know that God doesn't need your help, because *it's all already been done.*

Plus, here's the night-and-day difference between Abraham's situation and yours: Today, you're not waiting for God to make good on His promise. He already has! You're not waiting for Jesus to make you clean and close. He already has!

As a believer today, what you have is even better than what Abraham was offered. He was called to put his faith in a *future* event. You're called to put your faith in something that has already happened—the *finished* work of Jesus Christ!

CHASING THE MOUSE

We both have cats in our families. Andrew's cat's favorite toy is a stick with an elastic cord and a stuffed mouse tied on the end. The cat will drag the toy through the house, begging anyone to pick it up and play with him. And when you do, he goes wild! Chasing that mouse is his favorite thing in the world. He only catches it every once in a while, and when he does, it's soon whipped out of his mouth again, and the chase continues.

Some of us chase after experiences that give us satisfaction and that strong positive emotion of "catching the mouse"—a dramatic worship service, a campfire rededication, an inspiring conference, or a lengthy confession session before communion. These may give us a mountaintop experience, but it only lasts so long. Before we know it, we're right back where we started, or maybe even a bit lower. So we go dragging our emotions around, so to speak, searching for the next experience that will give us that high again. We're looking to feel okay once more. We want to feel closer to God. We want to feel restored to rightness.

Is this what God intended for us? No, this is trying to "do something" or "make something happen" rather than—by faith—practicing the art of doing nothing. This is us, just like Abraham, looking for ways we can "help" God rather than relying on what He already said is true.

Now, this is not to say there's anything wrong with heartfelt praise and worship, a good conference, or someone we can be transparent with. Those are all good things! But when we *rely* on that experience, and particularly when that experience involves getting "more" or achieving a "higher level" or "rededicating your efforts," then watch out!

It's a game of cat and mouse.

When we feel that we must experience something in order to be okay, the corollary is that we're not presently okay because we're not feeling okay. But this is a lie. The Gospel is not a promise that you will feel something. The Gospel is not an invitation to chase after more of Christ. The Gospel is an invitation to stop hungering and stop thirsting altogether, because we have been satisfied in Jesus (John 6:35).

It's an invitation—by faith—to practice the art of doing nothing.

> *But to **the one who does not work,** but believes in Him who justifies the ungodly, his faith is credited as righteousness.* (Romans 4:5)

EXPERIENCE-CHASING

Start a Daniel fast. Adopt the Sabbath. Pursue these disciplines. Practice this spiritual gift.

We're constantly offered new and trendy experiences to "enhance" our faith. We're exhorted to walk down the aisle at church to promise or commit or rededicate ourselves so we can feel renewed and clean. We're encouraged to sing the same song over and over again, engaging in repetitive behavior that psychologists have shown alleviates emotional stress. We're constantly drowning in instruction on new things we should do to be "more spiritual." Man-made religion inundates us with calls to find something deeper and experience something greater if we would just pursue the latest trend.

Any message of experience-chasing is an attack on our completeness in Christ. The enemy accuses us with: "What's wrong with you? If you were truly saved, you would feel more. If you were believing the truth, your emotions would be all healed up. You wouldn't waver so much!"

As humans, we love to feel. Positive emotions can put us on top of the world, while negative feelings can make us believe we're at the very bottom. But we also know that we can't trust our feelings. Emotions can come out of nowhere. They're not reliable. Most importantly, they often don't reflect what God says is true. There's nothing wrong with having feelings, but we don't want feelings to have us.

Now don't get us wrong: We're emotional creatures, and our emotions are designed to rise and fall, to ebb and flow. Of course! But the lie is that if you were truly experiencing the abundant life, then you would feel super spiritual and great all the time.

The truth is that it isn't about pursuing new emotions. It's about *the renewing of your mind* and learning as much as you can about the love and grace of God found in Christ Jesus (Romans 12:2; 2 Peter 3:18).

It's about *knowing* a Person.

Nothing to Chase

"Oh, yes, I've heard about this. Yes, I'm pursuing the abundant life! The victorious life! Yes, I'm learning to abide, to enter His rest, and to live on a higher plane above my circumstances!"

The abundant life in Christ is not something you pursue. Jesus came to give it to you, and He did (John 10:10). Victorious? God was already victorious over sin and death, and He made you dead to sin and alive to Him. The evil one cannot touch you (1 John 5:18). Abide? Abide simply means "to live," and you do live in Christ every day, all day long. Enter His rest? You've already entered His rest. Hebrews 4 speaks of this rest and invites unbelieving Jews to exit a spiritual wilderness and enter God's rest. You've done that, as you're in Christ now. Life on a higher plane? God already raised you up and seated you in heavenly places right next to Him (Ephesians 2:6).

So what if there's nothing to chase? What if you already have everything you need?

> Seeing that His divine power has granted to us **everything pertaining to life and godliness**, through the true knowledge of Him who called us by His own glory and excellence. (2 Peter 1:3)

> For in Him all the fullness of Deity dwells in bodily form, and **in Him you have been made complete,** and He is the head over all rule and authority. (Colossians 2:9–10)

YOU'RE OKAY

For many years, Andrew's grandfather had a license plate that read: IMOKRU. And that's the pitch so many religious leaders are selling: "I am okay. Are you okay like me?" Then they present the "method" of arriving at okayness.

But here's God's message to you: IMOKUR2.

Through Jesus Christ, you've been made okay (more than okay—righteous!). Because of your "okayness," you can finally get off the treadmill of self-improvement. You can cease your daily attempts to get clean and close and to get right and stay right. Even when you feel dirty and distant, you're invited to go with truth rather than emotion. The truth will always set you free, and it never disappoints!

*For the Scripture says, "Whoever believes in Him **will not be disappointed.**"* (Romans 10:11)

CHAPTER 22

Here's a portion of an email we received from a church leader who is just starting to practice the art of doing nothing. And already, it seems he's doing more than ever before!

> Hebrews clearly explains that Jesus died once for all—for everything and for everyone. When I read that, everything clicked into place for me. I always "knew" I was forgiven, but now I believe this is true because God said so!
>
> For the longest time, I've had these questions. Honestly, I've felt like these were questions that the enemy used to deceive me.
>
> However, I could never shake this feeling that I was NOT a bad person just because I didn't read

my Bible or pray every day or confess my sins enough. Sure, I may have been lazy, but I wasn't unforgiven. I had seen God answer my prayers, and I was bearing fruit even when I wasn't "chapter-a-daying-it."

Now, I see this internal struggle I have is a result of my experience with human relationships, not my relationship with God. I finally understand the concept of "we see our Heavenly Father like our earthly father." My first thought after wrecking the car has been "He's gonna kill me," not "Dad, help!"

What God has done with my walk during these last sixty days is nothing short of amazing. I am being set free and unleashed all at the same time. There is a fire inside me that hasn't been there since I first became a believer. It is so overwhelming, so wonderful, and so freeing! I still have questions, and I am sure there are still strongholds that need to be broken, but I see more of the Light.

What I am seeing is such good news. This is the Gospel! And what is interesting is that, as I let this sink in, I am spending more and more time in the Word and in prayer than I have in years.

I can see why many are scared of this teaching. It goes against everything they've been told since they were young. But the more people begin to realize this, the more they will read what the Bible actually says.

First, they need to understand where the new covenant begins. This is a big shift in their

thinking, but it's easy to get them there. Then, we can share with them that Jesus died—once for all. That will be where things get interesting!
—Bob

Our favorite part of Bob's letter is: "I am being *set free* and *unleashed* all at the same time." That's exactly what happens when we begin to really understand God's grace. We enjoy a newfound liberty in Jesus, yet it doesn't lead to passivity. We practice the art of doing nothing, but we may end up doing more than ever—without even trying.

How exactly do we practice this art of doing nothing? Over the next two chapters, we're going to revisit some aspects of the Gospel we've already celebrated and put the pieces together. As you'll see, all the energy you once used to try to get yourself right and then stay right with God can be redirected. You can know you're clean. You can know you're close. You can know you're qualified.

You are free to think in a new way ... because you're okay.

ASPECT #1:
DO NOTHING TO GET CLOSER TO GOD

What should we do to get closer to God? *Nothing.*

What? Yes, we know this may sound counterintuitive to you. It may even sound wrong. It may contradict what you've heard in a hundred sermons or read in other Christian books. But as we look into God's Word, we find that this is, in fact, the shocking and powerful reality: You're already as close to God as you can get.

1 Corinthians 6:17 says, "the one who joins himself to the Lord is one spirit with him." When did you join yourself to the Lord? At salvation, when you became the new-hearted, perfect you. So, you're now close to the Lord—spiritually bonded, connected, fused. You're as intimately connected as you could ever be. You just can't get any closer than "one spirit."

Many people speak of studying the Bible to get closer to God. What's really happening is they're filling and renewing their minds with God's truth. In so doing, they're learning about God's goodness, and their emotions respond. They *feel* good, because they're thinking good *thoughts.*

But this doesn't mean they're actually inching closer and closer to God over time. It simply means they're learning to set their mind on the truth, more and more (Colossians 3:2). But the truth (the reality) of their closeness was there all the while.

You read the Bible to get to know the Author. You read the Bible—not to get closer to Him—but to be reminded that you're *already* one spirit with Him.

God forgave you fully. He reconciled you completely. He joined you to Himself permanently. He crucified, buried, and raised you to newness of life. He raised and seated you with Him in heavenly places. So what do you need to do to get closer to God?

Nothing.

Instead, you can count on your perfect closeness. You can act on it. You can think that way and respond that way. But you can't do anything to add to what God has already done.

When you were dead in your transgressions and the
*uncircumcision of your flesh, **He made you alive***

*together with Him, having forgiven us all our trans-
gressions.* (Colossians 2:13)

"APPROPRIATE" IT?

Even the simple truth of your perfect closeness can be
misinterpreted. Perhaps nothing has caused more misunder-
standing than the idea of "appropriating" a truth like this.

Have you ever tried to "appropriate" a spiritual truth?
That's a really fine-sounding term—"appropriate"—which is
formally defined as "to take or make use of without authority
or right."

Wow. It suggests you're taking something that you have
no right to! As in an old TV show, you might think of a cop
on foot flashing his badge to commandeer a vehicle. In Christian contexts, it's usually defined this way: "to make real in
your own experience what God says is already true of you
positionally." This sounds a bit scholarly, and even somewhat
spiritual, but it still carries the same connotation: You don't
actually deserve "it" or have a right to "it" (whatever it is), but
you can somehow make use of it through an act of your will.

Well, let's give it a try. Yes, right now. Over the next fif-
teen seconds, why don't you appropriate your perfect closeness
with God? Actually, why not appropriate your forgiveness and
your righteousness too, while you're at it? Take a short break
in reading and give yourself a chance to do that. Go ahead.
Appropriate your closeness and forgiveness and righteousness.
Ready ... Go!

... Alright, now that you're back, how did it go? No, we're
not being sarcastic. We just want to make a point. Did you

appropriate your closeness with God? Your forgiveness? Your righteousness? How do you know you did it successfully? What is the indicator to measure your success? A feeling?

The bottom line is this: Words like "appropriate" sound good, but they don't make sense when taken to their ultimate conclusion. Truths like your closeness, your forgiveness, and your righteousness are just plain true. You don't need to do anything to make them truer. There's no "switch" you need to flick to "activate" something. You're perfectly close, perfectly forgiven, and perfectly righteous. As a new creation, these are the truth about you, whether you realize them or not, and whether you feel them or not.

ASPECT #2: DO NOTHING TO GET MORE FORGIVEN AND CLEANSED

If you've read this far in the book, then you've already seen the truth about your forgiveness: You're already totally forgiven of all your sins—past, present, and future (Hebrews 10:14). By Christ's one-time sacrifice, you've been perfectly cleansed "once for all." So, you don't have to "do anything" to get more forgiven or cleansed. Still, it's one thing to agree with this while you're reading our book. It's another to believe it in the midst of accusation.

Think of one thing you've done that you're particularly ashamed of—something from your past, something you've wrestled with, whether a habitual sin or a one-time occurrence. Now, in the moment that you're attacked by the Accuser and the evidence is playing on the movie screen of your mind, what do you do?

Do you seek to justify it with, "Well, not too many people got hurt"? Or perhaps with, "It only happened once"? Or even, "I will never do it again"?

While few people getting hurt or it only happening once or deciding to never do it again are all positive things, none of those results in your forgiveness. None of those is how God wants you to respond in the moment of accusation.

Instead, God is calling you to do nothing. *Nothing?* What would justify your doing nothing at all? Here's the idea: When you do nothing—providing no fleshly defense to accusation—you're actually counting yourself dead to that thought. You're simply not engaging with it.

You see, the enemy is like a whiny trial lawyer sitting on the courthouse steps trying to retry a case that has already been closed. Satan continually tempts you to return to the courtroom for more arguments, more debate, more defense. But it's all a charade. No attention to such matters is needed, not in the slightest. Why? Because "it is finished" (John 19:30).

So when you "do nothing" in response to such calls to defend your past sins, you aren't minimizing them. Exactly the opposite: You're respecting the finished work of Christ. You're agreeing that nothing further needs to be done on your behalf. You're honoring Jesus's sacrifice wholly and completely. You're agreeing with God that your sins are not taken into account and that they're remembered no more (Romans 4:8; Hebrews 10:17).

No One Else Like Him

Perhaps our problem in understanding our relationship with God is we're tempted to equate it with a human relationship. But the truth is there's just nothing like it. Nothing compares to what we have with God. We have a perfect "vertical" bond with Him that can't be broken or affected in the slightest by our performance.

Relating to other people is different, very different. Asking another person to forgive you for harming them makes it easier for them to forgive and for fellowship to be restored between you. That's the "horizontal" world we live in with others.

But the reason we can't equate the vertical with the horizontal is that in the latter, there was no blood sacrifice. No one else died for your sins. No one else took them away all at once. No one else fully understands that you've got a perfectly obedient heart that always regrets sin.

No one else can relate to you like Jesus can.

HORIZONTAL VERSUS VERTICAL

In the horizontal realm, you share your struggles with trusted friends (James 5:16) and gather with others for amazing community (Hebrews 10:25). This can be very encouraging for you, but it doesn't improve the vertical. The vertical connection you enjoy with God is perfect and permanent.

Think about it: If the vertical were not perfect and permanent, how would you ever effectively deal with the horizontal? The horizontal is hard enough—all that relating to other people, forgiving others, navigating challenging relationships—and it can be very taxing. Now, imagine trying to navigate the vertical with God at the same time!

Well … most of us don't have to imagine it, because that's the load we've tried to carry for so long. No wonder we end up exhausted, frustrated, and ultimately disillusioned. We were never designed to maintain the "vertical" and the "horizontal" at the same time. This is why in Christ, the vertical had to be accomplished, once for all.

Now, we're not saying all believers are fully grown. Of course not. You're continuously learning and getting your mind renewed. But even while you're learning and growing, your vertical relationship with God is at 100 percent. You're perfectly close and fully forgiven and righteous beyond measure, even while some of your thinking is immature. As you grow—and even as you make mistakes and commit sins—you never have to wonder about the condition of your vertical connection with God.

Consider that for a moment. What if you truly stopped all attempts to get right and stay right with God? What if you had all that energy back? What if you instead had energy to think about loving other people from a place of stability and rest? What might that do for you?

That's exactly the life that God has set up for you to enjoy! He has made it possible for you to take your eyes off of unwarranted fears about your spiritual condition and to look instead to the needs of others.

WHAT ABOUT FELLOWSHIP?

But don't we "fall out of fellowship" with God? Isn't that scriptural?

Actually, *no*. The term "fellowship" is never used that way in the New Testament. You're not going in and out of fellowship with God. Fellowship in the Bible refers to your "vertical" bond with God. That bond is never at 0 percent or even 64 percent. It's always at 100 percent. Because your sins have been taken away—once for all—and because you are "united with Christ" (Romans 6:5), your fellowship is perfect and permanent.

If you choose to sin, you have to do so *while* you're in fellowship with God. That's why it's not as fun as it used to be, right? Your union with Jesus is real. Your new heart is alive. Your new desires call out. Sin goes against the grain.

Just think about it: If you were not totally forgiven forever, then you'd have the Garden of Eden all over again. "Oh, you ate from the tree? Then get out of the garden!" You would die spiritually on Monday, and then again on Tuesday, and Wednesday, and every day.

Some people believe this. Yes, they literally believe they lose their salvation every time they sin. They believe when something happens in the horizontal, the vertical is then broken. But that's *not* the truth. You get to live the horizontal, knowing the vertical is perfect and permanent. You're totally forgiven and totally righteous all the time:

> For by one offering He has **perfected for all time** those who are sanctified. (Hebrews 10:14)

> He made Him who knew no sin to be sin on our behalf, so that **we might become the righteousness of God** in Him. (2 Corinthians 5:21)

CHAPTER 23

Go to the extreme. Don't hesitate to celebrate how clean and close you are to God. Don't let anyone water it down or put conditions on it. There's simply no room for compromise when it comes to God's perfect *agape* love. It's *that* amazing!

Make no mistake: The enemy is happy to sell you a lesser belief system specifically designed to erode your assurance and your confidence with God. Oh yes, he's delighted to offer you a list of actions and convince you that you need to do them all to "activate" what's already true for you.

This appeals to the flesh because on Planet Earth, we typically have to work before we can rest. We work throughout the week in order to rest on the weekend. We work throughout our lives in order to retire later. But Jesus offers us the opposite.

The Christian life *starts* with rest. We "work" from a place of *already* resting.

But what are you to do when you don't feel the closeness or the acceptance or the forgiveness of God? You can acknowledge those feelings and talk to God and others about them. However, the answer will still be the same—your feelings don't always line up with the truth.

Remember: It's about a *knowing*, not a feeling.

Maybe you grew up believing you had to go with your feelings or else you were acting like a hypocrite. You thought being true to your feelings was being true to yourself. But if you're a believer, those two are *not* the same much of the time! In fact, in order to be true to yourself—who you really are— you often need to go *against* your feelings.

Real hypocrisy is not going against your feelings. No, hypocrisy is acting in a way that's contrary to who you really are. So hypocrisy has nothing to do with your feelings. Quite often, your feelings will communicate one thing to you, yet you're called to do *the polar opposite* in order to be true to yourself: the new-hearted self that God made you.

ASPECT #3: DO NOTHING TO MONITOR OR FIX YOUR HEART

Some say your heart got hardened when you experienced that divorce. Others say it's the porn addiction you might still struggle with that has hardened your heart. Now God needs to soften your heart, but only if you'll let Him.

But is this the truth? No!

Sure, some of the attitudes and beliefs formed during that painful divorce may still linger in your mind. And some of those old thoughts from the porn addiction may plague you at times. But all of that is happening in the mental space, not in your heart. Your heart is as good and true today as it was on the day of salvation. So as a believer, while you experience a renewing of the mind, you can "do nothing" to fix your heart. It's already beyond changed—it's been exchanged!

Earlier, we asked the question, "How can we say we are good if Jesus said, 'No one is good except God alone'" (Mark 10:18)?

At that time, it was absolutely true. There was no one "good"—only God. But things are different today. Jesus died and rose again to make you good. Being born again makes a difference. You are born of God, born of the Spirit, and a slave of righteousness (Romans 6:18). You're good in a way that no one was before the cross (Luke 7:28). You're a new creation. You're a child of the living God. You're a partaker of His divine nature (2 Corinthians 5:17; 1 John 3:1; 2 Peter 1:4).

You might say, "Well, yes, that may be true ... in Christ. But we are nothing apart from Christ." Of course, that's a fact, but here's something to consider: Are you ever not in Christ? Are you ever apart from Him? No. So let's stop using false hypotheticals to diminish what He accomplished. His finished work is good, and you are now good.

Who you are will never change again. You're spiritually alive, and you'll never be dead. You're new-hearted, and you'll never be old-hearted. You're a child of God, and you'll never be a child of wrath. You're good, and you'll never be evil. So get used to it—you're in Christ forever. "In Christ" is your reality. The perfect you "in Christ" is the only you that you've got—and you're good!

WHAT ABOUT SANCTIFICATION?

Maybe you're thinking, *But haven't you forgotten about progressive sanctification? It seems like you're ignoring the tension between the "already" and the "not yet"!*

We hear you, but no, we believe the religious world has framed the whole "progressive sanctification" or "progressive holiness" thing wrongly. To sanctify (or to make holy) means "to set apart for a purpose." The Bible talks about two types of sanctification:

> Type 1: Sanctification (setting apart) of you as a person.
> Type 2: Sanctification (setting apart) of your attitudes and actions.

Distinguishing between identity and behavior is essential. When these two types of sanctification are conflated into one, all kinds of errors follow. That's exactly what has happened today, as the average person thinks they're being sanctified (or made holy) progressively with the improvement of their behavior. But that's not true!

We shouldn't conflate the two types of sanctification. To understand why, let's look at the first type of sanctification—of you as a person—in these passages that are often ignored:

*To open their eyes so that they may turn from darkness to light and from the dominion of Satan to God, that they may receive forgiveness of sins and an inheritance among **those who have been sanctified by faith in Me.*** (Acts 26:18)

*Such were some of you; but you were washed, but **you were sanctified**, but you were justified in the name of the Lord Jesus Christ and in the Spirit of our God.* (1 Corinthians 6:11)

*By this will **we have been sanctified** through the offering of the body of Jesus Christ once for all.* (Hebrews 10:10)

Did you notice that, in all three passages, it says you have been (or were) sanctified—past tense? You as a person have *already* been fully set apart for God. God Himself did the setting apart, and you can't improve upon that. You're a person of God's own possession (1 Peter 2:9). You're 100 percent reserved for God. It's not progressive. If Jesus Christ were to return for you right now, you would fully belong to Him. After all, He's not coming for a portion of you. He embraces all of you!

Now, notice the second kind of sanctification (or holiness) expressed in this passage:

*But like the Holy One who called you, **be holy** yourselves also **in all your behavior.*** (1 Peter 1:15)

Here, Peter is talking about your behavior. That's the
progressive part. The setting apart of your attitudes and
actions is a work in progress. It's ongoing. But you—as a
person—have already been set apart fully and forever.

We need to keep these two types of sanctification separate:
us versus *our behavior.* Our attitudes and actions don't define us
or determine our set-apartness. If we're not careful, we'll find
ourselves saying we don't believe in works-based righteousness
while still buying the lie of works-based holiness!

Remember that whatever God did to you to make you His
own, it all happened at the same time:

> *Such were some of you; but you were **washed**, but you
> were **sanctified**, but you were **justified** in the name of
> the Lord Jesus Christ and in the Spirit of our God.* (1
> Corinthians 6:11)

You were washed and justified *and sanctified* at the exact
same time. So we're not "ignoring sanctification" as we discuss
the perfect you. We're simply separating who we are from
what we do, just as the Gospel message itself does.

Here's a snapshot of how what we're saying differs from
the popular view:

	the "already"	the "not yet"
popular view	justification of <u>you</u>	"progressive sanctification" of <u>you</u> via your behavior (conflated view)
biblical view	justification and sanctification of <u>you</u>	sanctification of your behavior (this doesn't make <u>you</u> "better")

CLARIFYING GROWTH

Here's why all of this is so important: There's a subtle yet powerful form of rejection heaped on believers, whether we realize it or not. It's the idea that growth causes a change in our spiritual makeup (not merely our attitudes and actions) that makes us more acceptable to God over time. This is a damaging lie that often goes undetected.

To clear this up, let's state the truth a few different ways:

1. You are perfectly forgiven, perfectly righteous, and perfectly set apart for God even if you never grow or learn anything else about Him.
2. You are 100 percent Heaven-ready right now if Christ were to return in this moment. No last-minute polish of you is needed. You'll simply leave behind the sinful influencers (the world, the flesh, and the power of sin), and that is enough. There's nothing wrong with who you are.
3. God doesn't love and accept *only* a spiritual compartment of you. He loves and accepts all of you—spirit, soul, and body. Your spirit is joined to His. Your soul (personality) goes to Heaven too, with no last-minute cleansing needed. Even though you'll get a new resurrection body, your current body is the temple of the Holy Spirit (1 Corinthians 6:19), and it, too, is holy and acceptable to God (Romans 12:1).

In short, there's no part of you that needs fixing before God will delight in you. He already does in every way. Yes, you're learning to reflect (in the "mirror" of your soul) more and more who you really are at the core. But this doesn't make *you* any better. Your intrinsic newness and righteousness remain the same, even as you learn and grow in your attitudes and actions.

ASPECT #4: DO NOTHING TO FEEL MORE

God never calls us to feel. He calls us to *know*. 1 John 5:13 says, "I've written to you who believe in the name of the Son of God so that you may *know* that you have eternal life." Notice that it doesn't say "so that you may feel." We're never promised that we'll feel something. We're only assured that we can know something.

So whatever you might think Christian leaders, pastors, missionaries, or other spiritual leaders are feeling all the time, they're simply not. We're all human, and our feelings are all over the place. We drink a cup of coffee, and we feel energetic for a few hours. The end of the day arrives, and we feel fatigued. We eat bad food, and we feel indigestion. We feel all kinds of things, but it's the truth of who we are that sets us apart from the world:

> *"Sanctify them [set them apart] in the **truth**; Your word is truth."* (John 17:17)

We are excited—not about what we feel, but about what we know. We're excited about what Jesus has done. That's fact, not feeling.

Nevertheless, like you, we hear the sales pitches. *Adopt this belief, and you'll feel terrific. If you will tithe 10 percent, you'll feel*

God move you into a blessing. Keep the Sabbath, and you'll feel
spiritual rest. Take the Lord's Supper at home regularly, and you'll
feel blessed. You can have visions and dreams and be mightily used
by God if you would just give yourself over to this or that belief.
On and on the sales pitches go, and most of them are just
garbage. Here's what Paul had to say about these pitches:

> **Let no one keep defrauding you of your prize** *by*
> *delighting in self-abasement and the worship of the*
> *angels, taking his stand on visions he has seen,* **inflated**
> **without cause by his fleshly mind.** (Colossians 2:18)

Defrauding you of what prize? The prize of contentment
found in knowing that the perfect you—joined to Jesus—is
enough.
You don't have to go shopping for more "experiences."
Even if someone else is experiencing something from God,
you can wish them well but not believe the lie that you need
to experience the same in order to be okay:

> *For we are not bold* **to class or compare ourselves** *with*
> *some of those who commend themselves; but when they*
> **measure** *themselves by themselves and* **compare** *them-*
> *selves with themselves, they are* **without understand-**
> **ing.** (2 Corinthians 10:12)

When you idolize others and compare yourself, you're
acting without good understanding of the Gospel message.
We've all looked over at someone in church who has their
hands raised high, who's swaying back and forth, who's

looking up to Heaven with a very sincere and worshipful expression on their face. At that moment, you have two choices: (a) compare your own "experience" with their "experience" or (b) remember to be satisfied that you are complete, lacking nothing, and blessed with every spiritual blessing—no matter what body posture or facial expression you might display.

When you have your eyes fixed on others, they're not fixed on Jesus. In those moments, you feel that you're not complete and you're not enough. But you can take those thoughts captive (2 Corinthians 10:5) and choose to believe that you *are* complete in Jesus and He has made you enough.

You can practice the art of doing nothing to feel more.

WHAT CAN YOU DO?

There are plenty of things that you can do. You wake up every day, and you offer your body to Jesus. You walk by the Spirit. You set your mind. You love others. You grow in your knowledge of the Gospel. You thank God for all that He's done. You learn how to act like who you really are.

But these decisions can take place as your mind is clear and not preoccupied with the religious distractions:

- Trying to get closer to God
- Trying to get more forgiven and cleansed
- Trying to fix our hearts
- Trying to feel or "experience" more

In this way, you can practice the art of doing nothing to get right and stay right with God. In this way, you honor the finished work of Jesus Christ.

PART 9

THE PERFECT GOD

Chapter 24

There's even more that allows *the perfect you* to thrive. Your concept of God shapes and influences you more than you imagine. It frames your attitudes and your actions, even your responses to what may come your way. If you think God is harsh and vengeful, you may interpret difficult circumstances as His judgment upon you. If you think of God as demanding and unforgiving, you may interpret tough times as His retribution for your sins.

The way you view God informs your thought life, too. After all, who has confidence around an angry God who's eager to punish you as soon as you mess up? And if you believe your closeness with God can be hurt by your actions, you'll spend your life feeling dirty and distant from Him. You'll see Him as largely disappointed and rarely pleased with you.

You'll see Him being only as good to you as you are to Him.

When life is going well, have you ever asked, "I wonder when the hammer will drop?" Have you ever thought, "God, You're not going to let it be this smooth for too long! I'm sure You've got something coming through the side door. You're going to wreck me, or break me, or teach me a lesson soon. There's no way You're as good as You say!"

This indictment against God's perfect goodness can even seem valid, given the world we live in with its pain, suffering, tragedy, and injustice. We ask, "How could a good God let these things happen?"

That's why it's so important to get this right. You've got to know God for who He really is. An atmosphere of covenant-based forgiveness and grace will only take you so far. Deep within the recesses of your mind, you must believe that *the Author* of the covenant Himself is inherently good and can be fully trusted.

To say that God is good doesn't answer *all* your questions. There's still plenty of mystery unsolved. But God's goodness is not meant to be mysterious. He has declared His goodness and demonstrated it through Jesus (Romans 5:8). He is what He says He is.

He is perfectly good.

GOD'S GOODNESS MATTERS

Why is knowing God is good so important? It allows you to hold on to the certainty of His character in the midst of an uncertain world. You can trust His heart even when you don't understand His ways.

*"For My thoughts are not your thoughts, **nor are your ways My ways**," declares the Lord. "For as the heavens are higher than the earth, so are My ways **higher** than your ways, and My thoughts than your thoughts."* (Isaiah 55:8–9)

God's doesn't call you to understand Him *first* and trust Him *second*. No, you're called to trust God *first*. You are to trust Him, not necessarily understand Him. You are to know Him, not try to figure Him out. And when you choose to believe God is good, you're aligning your beliefs with the truth of who He really is.

And consider this: If God were not good, we'd lose our basis for anything to be good. The only reason we even recognize something is good is because we judge it by a standard. The ultimate, unchanging standard is God Himself.

In the Garden of Eden, Adam rejected God as the basis for his goodness. In a sense, Adam thumbed his nose at God and said, "I don't need Your goodness." Adam didn't know he was doing that, because he was deceived. Still, he decided in disobedience: "I will determine what's good and evil for myself. I don't need You to do that for me."

Adam ate of the tree and thereby chose to look to his own conscience to judge good and evil. To this very day, the world continues to decide what's "right" and "wrong" in their own estimation. Truth and goodness have become subjective. Likewise, humanity's "eating of that tree" has resulted in chaos and conflict as more and more people create and consult their own moral compasses.

And for this we blame God? He's the One who told us not to eat from that tree!

WHERE IS GOD IN CRISIS?

9/11. Hurricane Katrina. Coronavirus. It seems every time we face a disaster, some religious leaders take to the airwaves to proclaim that it's God's judgment upon the world. According to them, God was angry at New York City, then New Orleans, and now the whole planet.

As cases of coronavirus began to rise across the southern United States, state officials hosted a phone call for us pastors to discuss how to deal with the pandemic. Just a few minutes into the call, one pastor quoted James 5:16 and said we needed to begin confessing our sins one to another. Another urged us all to consider 1 John 1:9 and confess our sins to God in order to get right with Him. Several more implied that our sins were standing in the way of our prayers for the healing of our nation. God had brought the virus to "grab our attention," one claimed. "It's a scourge of discipline," another said.

The consensus was that God was hurling disaster at us because of our sins, and the solution was clear: Get right with God, and He will stop this. Fail to get right with God, and He will continue bludgeoning the world with it.

Does this view really hold up? Let's take a look at the truth about God and the disasters that strike our fallen world. What we find in the New Testament is very different from popular religious opinions today.

PERFECT GOD, PERFECT MOTIVES

God's goal isn't to kill people or to make them sick as a judgment for sin or to force them to listen to Him. No, He is seeking to save anyone and everyone who will call upon His name (Romans 10:13). Here's what the Apostle Peter wrote about God's agenda in the world today:

> *The Lord is not slow in keeping his promise, as some understand slowness. Instead he is patient with you, **not wanting anyone to perish, but everyone to come to repentance.*** (2 Peter 3:9 NIV)

God is not wishing for anyone to die. He wants every single person to turn and believe in Him. The Apostle Paul expressed it this way:

> *This is good, and pleases **God our Savior, who wants all people to be saved** and to come to a knowledge of the truth.* (1 Timothy 2:3–4 NIV)

So when disasters hit, what do you believe God is thinking about the world? Is He up in Heaven declaring, "I'm angry with you, so I'm hurling down trouble to punish you. Then, I'll punish you again for your sins at the final judgment"? Or is He saying, "I love you so much that I sent My Son to die for you and offer you new life in Him. I'm deeply concerned for you in the midst of what you're experiencing right now. I grieve along with you, and I want to be your Comforter, your Counselor, and your Life through this and all tragedies"?

Still, you might be tempted to think—like those pastors on the phone call—*Maybe God brings disaster upon us to drive more people toward repentance.* But here's what God's Word says about how He *really* leads people to repent:

> Or do you think lightly of the riches of His kindness and tolerance and patience, not knowing that **the kindness of God leads you to repentance?** (Romans 2:4)

Notice it's the kindness of the Lord that brings people to repent. God isn't trying to threaten or scare anyone into repentance. No, it's God's *goodness* that leads people to Him, and it's the *grace* of God that teaches us to say "no" to sin (Titus 2:11–12).

Look to Jesus!

If you really want to understand God in the midst of any crisis, you should—as always—*look to Jesus.* After all, Jesus said this about Himself:

> *Anyone who has seen Me has seen the Father. How can you say, "Show us the Father"?* (John 14:9b NIV)

So, if you've seen Jesus, then you've seen the Father. There's just no doubt about it: Jesus and the Father are on the exact same page. The author of Hebrews puts it this way:

> **The Son is** *the radiance of God's glory and* **the exact representation of his being,** *sustaining all things by his powerful word.* (Hebrews 1:3a NIV)

Jesus shows you exactly what God's agenda looks like. You look to the Son to understand the Father. And what do you discover about the Son, and therefore God's agenda in the world today? The Apostle John's words leave you with little room for doubt:

> *For God did **not** send his Son into the world **to condemn the world, but to save the world** through him.* (John 3:17 NIV)

And Jesus Himself clarified His mission in saying this:

> *If anyone hears My sayings and does not keep them, I do not judge him; **for I did not come to judge the world, but to save the world.*** (John 12:47)

If you want to understand the Father, you look to the Son. And it's clear from Jesus's own statements that God is on a mission to save the world, not to bring disaster upon it. This also bears out when you see how Jesus interacted with people during His earthly ministry. Not once did He strike people with illness. In fact, He did the polar opposite:

> *While the sun was setting, **all those who had any who were sick with various diseases** brought them to Him; and laying His hands on each one of them, **He was healing them.*** (Luke 4:40)

So where does all the trouble, sickness, and death come from, if not from God? It comes from the fallen world we live in. Here, Jesus contrasts what God desires for you against what the world brings:

> *I have told you these things, so that **in Me you may have peace. In this world you will have trouble.** But take heart! I have overcome the world.* (John 16:33 NIV)

Notice what Jesus brings you is peace in Him. The trouble doesn't come from Him but from the world. You can take Jesus at His word that His agenda with you is perfectly good. Our God is not two-faced. He's not hurling disaster at you and then pretending to comfort you in it later.

A Popular Passage

The most popular Bible passage that religious leaders refer to during times of disasters seems to be this one:

> ***If** my people, who are called by my name, will humble themselves and pray and seek my face and turn from their wicked ways, **then** I will hear from heaven, and I will forgive their sin and will heal their land.* (2 Chronicles 7:14 NIV)

Many have applied this passage to situations we've faced in the United States and around the world. In one way or another, they've implied that terrorism, or hurricanes, or coronavirus were America's fault or even the Church's fault. They've implied that if we would seek God more and obtain forgiveness for our sins, then God would heal our land of the problem.

However, it's a big mistake to apply this passage in that way. Why? Because it's an Old Testament passage, and we live in New Testament times. In the same passage, the Israelites are seen getting their sins forgiven by sacrificing 22,000 oxen and 120,000 sheep and consecrating the Temple that Solomon built. Israel lived under the Law, and God related to them through the old covenant. Their sins were covered through the shedding of animal blood.

Remember that we believers are not under the Law. We are under God's grace. We don't go to the Temple. We are the temple of the Holy Spirit. We don't have to live under the Law's 613 commands, and we're not sacrificing animals for our sins. Why not? Because Jesus fulfilled the Law through His once-for-all sacrifice. He is the perfect, spotless Lamb of God offered for our sins. And because of His sacrifice, we have been perfectly forgiven for all time:

> For *by one offering He has perfected for all time* those who are sanctified. (Hebrews 10:14)

Today, we live under a new covenant, a better covenant. We have a better sacrifice. And we have a better high priest, Jesus Christ. So it's wrong to apply the 2 Chronicles 7 passage to a terrorist attack or a natural disaster or the death of a loved one as a diagnosis of the cause or as a recipe for the solution. God was addressing the Israelites as they were living under the Law thousands of years ago, before the cross of Christ. We're reading someone else's mail in 2 Chronicles 7.

Someone else's mail? Yes, remember that we believers *already* have all the forgiveness we need in Jesus. Furthermore, we don't need to "seek His face" if we've already found Him (Matthew 7:7). Jesus said once we had Him, we'd never need to hunger or thirst for more (John 6:35). As believers, we already have Jesus, and therefore we have everything we need (2 Peter 1:3).

So the new covenant message we can share with the world today is not about a God who is launching trouble at them. No, it's about a God who loves them and longs to save them.

> *The Lord is ...* **not wishing for any to perish** *but for all to come to repentance.* (2 Peter 3:9)

> *Now is the time of God's favor,* **now is the day of salvation**. (2 Corinthians 6:2b NIV)

CHAPTER 25

As we've seen, God is not striking the world for its sins. Instead, our message to those around us is that God's desire is to reconcile them in Christ:

> *All this is from God, who reconciled us to himself through Christ and* **gave us the ministry of reconciliation:** *that God was reconciling the world to himself in Christ,* **not counting people's sins against them.** *And he has committed to us the message of reconciliation. We are therefore Christ's ambassadors, as though God were making his appeal through us.* **We implore you on Christ's behalf: Be reconciled to God.** (2 Corinthians 5:18–20 NIV)

Do we tell people that God is hurling disaster at them to get their attention, or do we tell them that He loves them and wants a relationship with them? The Apostle Paul is very clear: It's the latter!

After all, shouldn't the cross of Christ affect our view when disaster strikes? Doesn't the cross matter as we seek to understand who God is and what He's doing in the midst of a nightmare scenario? Of course it matters.

There are already great fears and much anxiety among many in our world. The last thing we believers should do is show up on the scene during trouble to heap guilt on others. Because of the cross and resurrection, the offer of forgiveness and new life is on the table. That's the grace-filled message we carry:

> *He has made us competent as ministers of a new covenant*—*not of the letter but of the Spirit; for the letter kills, but the Spirit gives life.* (2 Corinthians 3:6 NIV)

CHRISTIAN KARMA?

Terror. Sickness. Disaster. Death. These are not God's judgment on the world. Still, "Christian Karma"—the idea that the price for our sins is some trial or pandemic—seems to be rampant today. But it's a lie. The cross of Christ destroyed all karma. God wants to save the world, not to hurl plagues at it. (Yes, we know there were plagues in the Old Testament, and we'll address that soon!)

How do we know what God feels about the world? The Bible tells us where to look if we want to find God's love clearly demonstrated:

*But God **demonstrates his own love** for us in this:*
*While we were still sinners, **Christ died for us.***
(Romans 5:8 NIV)

If we want to see what God feels about the world, we should look to Jesus on the cross. This is God's clearest demonstration of His love. He didn't want there to be any doubt about His feelings for the world, so He sent His Son to give His very life for us (John 3:16). This is how much we are worth to God: We are worth Jesus!

THE END IS CLEAR!

Even as we were writing this book, there were many claiming that coronavirus might be the end of the world. So how do we know this is *not* the end of the world?

Because you don't stop God's judgment with a vaccine. You don't stop God's judgment with a pill. You don't stop God's judgment by closing your borders or staying indoors for a few months. If the coronavirus pandemic were truly God's judgment, humanity would not be able to prevent it or diminish it in the slightest.

But by His word the present heavens and earth are being
***reserved** for fire, **kept** for the day of judgment and*
destruction of ungodly men. (2 Peter 3:7)

There will be a day of judgment in the future, and it will not be stopped. But today is not that day.

Think about it. If a pandemic like coronavirus were God's judgment, then we apparently possess the power to stop God, or at least slow Him down. Furthermore, if it were from God, then He must be angriest with senior citizens who are the most susceptible. Also, if it were from God, then shouldn't we be praying for its spread? After all, as believers, we would want to work with God's plan, not against it!

Do you see how foolish it is for anyone to claim that these natural disasters are God's judgment on the world? Nevertheless, some people carry on saying this is God's discipline or God "getting our attention."

Imagine if you disciplined your own children or "got their attention" by injecting them with a lethal virus. You would (and should) be reported to Child Protective Services! Still, many project this sort of behavior onto our God and Father and entertain the idea that this is how He treats His children. This is not God's *agape* love for us. This is not the truth that sets us free!

Imagine you're a parent. You love your child, and you see him playing in a dangerous street. You explain why it's not safe to play there. You even call him inside when you see him disobeying you. So what do you do if he continues to disregard your warnings? Do you get in your car and try to run him down as a punishment for not obeying? No, right? That would be appalling! No loving parent would do something so barbaric. Yet, tragically, this is how many view God. They see Him as vengeful and vindictive, always looking to teach them a lesson, no matter the cost. Is that really how the "God of all comfort" (2 Corinthians 1:3) treats you?

TODAY: THE DAY OF SALVATION

Now, it's true that the Old Testament is filled with examples of judgment from God upon people as a result of their disobedience. The Flood, the destruction of Sodom and Gomorrah, the plagues of Egypt, and many other events are examples of how God inflicted physical punishment, including disasters and diseases, for sin. That's obvious.

We also read that, at the end of the age, whoever does not receive Christ will undergo judgment for their sins. We see this in Revelation 20 and in Matthew 25, for example. This, too, is obvious.

However, the question today is not: "Is the Old Testament filled with judgment of sin?" or "Is there a future day of judgment?" The answer to both of those questions is clearly, *yes*.

The question today is this: "Is God striking people with disaster as a judgment for sin?" And the answer to that is a definitive *no*. Even the earthly consequences of our own actions are *not* God's judgment upon us. Today is the day of salvation, not the Day of Judgment (2 Corinthians 6:2).

Yes, the Day of Judgment is coming, but *today is not that day*. We live in an era when we need to be proclaiming the Gospel that saves, not preaching God-given disasters that kill.

THE DAY OF JUDGMENT

When the Day of Judgment finally comes, you—as a believer—can eagerly await it, knowing that God will not refer to your sins.

*Truly, truly, I say to you, **he who hears My word, and believes Him who sent Me,** has eternal life, and **does not come into judgment,** but has passed out of death into life.* (John 5:24)

Remember, God already took away your sins as far as the east is from the west (Psalm 103:12). He remembers your sins no more (Hebrews 10:17).

*And inasmuch as it is appointed for men **to die once and after this comes judgment,** so Christ also, having been offered once to bear the sins of many, will appear a second time for salvation **without reference to sin, to those who eagerly await Him.*** (Hebrews 9:27–28)

Notice here that judgment comes after death, not before. That matters when so many are claiming that disasters on Earth today are God's judgment upon people before their death. According to the author of Hebrews, that's not the case!

When the Day of Judgment arrives, we believers can have complete confidence. God's perfect love casts away all our fear.

*By this, love is perfected with us, so that **we may have confidence in the day of judgment;** because **as He is, so also are we in this world.** There is no fear in love; but perfect love casts out fear, because fear involves punishment, and **the one who fears is not perfected in love.*** (1 John 4:17–18)

The one who fears imagines punishment on the Day of Judgment. But as children of God, we can be *excited* about that day. John assures us that we have nothing to worry about. We can know for certain that we're as safe as Jesus at the Final Judgment.

Why? Because God is good.

FALLEN WORLD, SOVEREIGN GOD

If God does not bring disaster as judgment on the world, then where does it come from? If you've lived a day on this planet, you've probably noticed the terrible things that happen: accidents, violence, rape, murder, riots, and hate. They happen every day in this fallen world, but God is not the author of any of those things.

God is not the author of sin and death, nor is He the author of disease and suffering. God is the author and perfecter of our faith (Hebrews 12:2). God does not cause all things, but He does cause all things to work together for good for those who love Him (Romans 8:28).

God is not a death-dealer. He is a life-giver!

Okay, but doesn't God's sovereignty come into play here? If we simply blame disasters on the fallen world, aren't we threatening God's sovereignty? Those questions can be addressed with even more questions like these: *Was God's sovereignty threatened when Satan rebelled? Was God's sovereignty threatened when Adam and Eve sinned against Him? Is God's sovereignty threatened each time people all over the Earth choose to sin?*

Of course not. That would be a pathetic kind of sovereignty!

God created angels and humans with a choice. Because His sovereignty is not threatened, He created people with the freedom to love Him or rebel against Him. That's what true love is all about—having a choice to respond. It's not robotic. It doesn't happen by force.

Consider this: Which God is more sovereign—the One who must control our every move lest His authority and plan be threatened? Or the One who reigns supreme and whose plan is not thwarted by our choices?

THE PRICE OF SIN

Lastly, when we imagine that disasters are God's wrath or judgment, we diminish the importance of the cross itself. Remember that the wages of sin is death (Romans 6:23). Not illness, not suffering, not difficulty: The wages of sin is nothing short of *death* for anyone and everyone.

But Jesus died. He took the wages in full. So we can do the math and celebrate!

Yes, His sacrifice on the cross canceled our debt in full. Now, there's nothing left to pay. Because "it is finished," we've been forgiven of our sins and freed from all punishment. Through the cross, we're saved from wrath (Romans 5:9). And there is no condemnation for those of us who are in Jesus Christ (Romans 8:1).

Not only did God completely forgive us of all our sins, but He also gifted us with a new and never-ending life in Him:

When you were dead in your sins and the uncircumcision of your flesh, **God made you alive. He forgave us all our sins.** (Colossians 2:13 NIV)

Taste and See That the Lord Is Good!

We live in a fallen world. In this world, we see sin, disaster, and suffering of all kinds. As a result of the fall of humanity, we also see flawed DNA, disease, and death. But God did not author these. None of these existed in Eden, and they will not exist in Heaven.

God created a perfect world. It was only when we humans decided to take matters into our own hands that the world became imperfect. God is still good, even when our fallen world sends disaster our way. God is still good even while we reap the earthly consequences of poor choices we and others make.

Yes, God is good. So we can give thanks to God for every *good* thing (James 1:17). But where does all the *bad* in this world come from? There are many factors at work: the fallen world in general; the enemy, Satan; the power of sin; and the flesh.

Here's the healthy distinction we must arrive at: Planet Earth comes at us to attack us and bring us down. Christ works in us to love us and build us up in Him (Colossians 2:7). Even His discipline is always an act of love as He trains us for the future. He never punishes us for the past.

We believers are invited to comfort each other in the process. God tells us to "grieve with those who grieve"

(Romans 12:15). Is this not what God Himself is doing with us as we go through hard times?

He cares.

God is our Counselor, our Comforter, and our Helper in times of distress. It's essential that we remember this when we encounter trouble. We need to know God's love, which is found in Jesus Christ. The God who is good, the God of all comfort—this is our God.

> *O taste and see that the Lord is good; blessed is the man who takes **refuge** in him!* (Psalm 34:8)

> *Praise be to the God and Father of our Lord Jesus Christ, the Father of compassion and **the God of all comfort, who comforts us in all our troubles, so that we can comfort those in any trouble** with the comfort we ourselves receive from God.* (2 Corinthians 1:3–4 NIV)

PART 10

LIVING AS THE PERFECT YOU

CHAPTER 26

Once you embrace the perfect you and the reality of a perfectly good God, it begins to affect the way you see yourself and other people. These precious truths become instrumental in healing relationships of all kinds—friendships, marriages, family relationships, and more.

PEOPLE CLOSE TO YOU

The better you know someone, the more tempting it is to try to change them. As for a casual acquaintance at work, you might just wish they wouldn't feel the need to chat so much, or maybe you wish they would be more friendly. But the closer you get to someone—a relative, a child, a spouse—the more you might expect them to think and act like you want them to.

You have expectations for others, and each time they fail to meet them, you may grow frustrated with their performance. And the more frustrated you are, the more emotions build up inside you. Perhaps you try to manipulate them into changing, or shame them, or get revenge in small ways, or even lash out at times in resentment. Or you might bottle it up within you until, like a pressure cooker, it gets to be too much, and you explode.

But let's back up a step and understand where all this is coming from. It's because you've bought into the fleshly lie that it is your job to "fix" them or to make them more like you, or more like a standard you have for how people should behave. This creates a conflict inside you that you're simply not meant to bear.

If that's the problem, then what's the solution? Exactly what we've been talking about in this book: understanding the new-hearted, perfect you and God's love and acceptance of you. Then you can be yourself and begin to release others to be themselves as well.

> *Therefore,* **accept one another,** *just as Christ also accepted us to the glory of God.* (Romans 15:7)

Just as you've learned to trust your own new heart, you can begin to trust the new hearts of believers around you and trust the good God who lives in them. And as for unbelievers, you can trust God with them too, instead of playing God for them.

A new-covenant perspective offers new insight into how to relate to your spouse, your family members, and your friends.

"FIXING" VERSUS ACCEPTING

One of the biggest unwritten assumptions as you enter new relationships is that the other person needs to be *improved*. Of course, you already think they're great. (Otherwise, why would you want to get closer to them?) But the more you get to know someone, the more you think: "If only they did this, or acted more like I think they should, then they'd really be perfect."

But remember: If they're a new-hearted self, then they're already perfect, no matter what they might reflect with their "soul mirror" at times. They're designed to be loved, not fixed. (This goes for the unbeliever too, as even God does not "fix" them as much as He makes them brand new.)

Maybe you aren't even quite conscious of your erroneous belief that you can change them. And they're likely unaware of your plans too, even if they have similar goals for you to "improve" as well. Regardless, as the relationship grows and matures, you often find out—one way or another—you cannot seem to change them. Your frustration, your disapproval, and even your judgment then communicates the opposite of what you want in a relationship. Instead of growing closer, you start to grow apart.

You begin to believe that they are the problem when they're not. Sometimes you let them convince you that *you* are the problem, when you're actually not. The reality is that each of us, as believers, shares a common enemy that can distort our vision of the other person. *The power of sin is that common enemy. The power of sin is the real problem.*

*For our struggle is **not against flesh and blood**, but against the rulers, against the powers, against the world*

forces of this darkness, against the spiritual forces of
wickedness in the heavenly places. (Ephesians 6:12)

As a believer, you have a choice: Will your soul reflect
your new heart? Or will it reflect the sinful flesh patterns
learned from the world? You're often tempted to express sin,
and when you do, all too often those closest to you bear its
brunt. Not only that, but sin can skew your perspective. You
begin to see others in a way that's not reflective of who they
are. Sometimes it's not that something is wrong with them.
It's only your perspective of them that's the problem.

What's the solution? The solution is to choose to see them
how God does. And the reason you can do this is because you
have a new heart, and so do they! So how would your attitudes
and actions change if you viewed those around you as the
new-hearted, perfect selves that they are? *Rather than viewing*
them as not measuring up, what if you saw them as people who
sometimes fail to express their true identity?

Let Them Be!

The new-covenant perspective inspires you to let people
be. If you're a new-hearted, perfect self, then you can trust
God with every aspect of who they are too. It's not up to you
to fix them anymore. It's not your responsibility. Your role is
to choose what the mirror of your own soul will reflect toward
them in any given moment.

Of course, lending a helping hand or receptive ear is part
of what makes up a good relationship. That's an important
way you can demonstrate love to each other and reflect your

new identity. But sometimes the desire to "help" doesn't originate with the other person's requesting it or wanting it. For
example, if your spouse or best friend is silent for a period of
time, you may assume the worst. You may decide they're
angry with you and that you need to "fix" the situation.

Now, it may only be that they're deep in thought or men-
tally exhausted from a long day or they just aren't as talkative
as you are to begin with. They simply don't want to engage
right now. Not everyone is an extrovert!

Nevertheless, the power of sin whispers to you that this is
surely a bad sign and that you must "rescue" everything. You
make yourself "okay" by forcing them to talk about what is
bothering them and then fixing it. This can actually lead to
a conflict when *there was no original issue to start with!*

Here's how it might look:

You: *What's wrong?*

Friend/Spouse: *Nothing.*

You: *No, really. What's wrong? Let's talk about it.*

Friend/Spouse: *I said "nothing." I'm just tired.*

You: *Why won't you ever talk to me?*

Friend/Spouse: *Maybe because it's always like this!*

(Result: Both parties are hurt and angry when there really
wasn't a problem.)

This is just one example of how we can assume the worst.
But 1 Corinthians 13:7 says "love believes all things." So it's
already on your new, loving heart to "believe all things" about
the other person, and that means assuming the best about
them.

Maybe they're quiet because they're mulling things over
from their day. They may be strategizing, thinking over how

to respond to a situation. Or they may simply be withdrawing to recharge. So how can you love them in that circumstance? Instead of worrying, give them the freedom, acceptance, and space they need.

It may be that they don't want to communicate right then. Let them communicate in their timing. But you can still show that you care: "Let me know if I can do anything for you. I'm here for you" could be more helpful than "Tell me what's wrong. Why won't you talk to me?"

Of course, it's not about any exact words to memorize and deliver. It's ultimately about giving them the love and respect they desire. It's about caring for them from the heart!

DON'T SOLVE EVERY "PROBLEM"

Here's another example of when you can "let them be." Sometimes they're sharing their feelings and—rather than listening and empathizing—you jump in to "fix" those feelings or "help" them. Here again, the unintended result could be *rejection*. Here's an example:

Friend/Spouse: *My boss is impossible. I worry that he doesn't like me.*

You: *You're always negative and stressed out.*

Friend/Spouse: *Well, it is stressful in that place. I'm not sure if I can do the job!*

You: *Remember Sunday's sermon: You can do all things through Christ.*

Friend/Spouse: *Why can't I ever really talk to you?*

(Result: You feel unable to help. They feel emotionally abandoned. There's even a bit of religious judgment thrown in for not being "strong" enough in faith.)

Here, they are sharing what is going on in their life, and you label them as negative and stressed. Then you're tempted to get on a soapbox and start preaching a bit! You start trying to teach them a spiritual lesson as they're sharing about their day. Now it feels like the God of the Universe is coming down on them for their feelings: "You don't need to be so fearful all the time. Don't you remember what Pastor Jim said on Sunday?"

This is a good example of what happens when we try to jump in and fix the other person. And we wonder why they don't love it when we're trying to remedy their problem? Rather than recognizing the need for listening and understanding, we end up seeing the other person as a project to complete rather than a person to love. This is rejection at its finest!

Conversely, sometimes there's no interaction at all when there should be. One person is in the pit of despair, and we think it's respectful to "give space." But space is not what's really needed. The one in despair wants to share and be heard. So they take our silence as meaning we don't care about their thoughts and needs.

Again, there is no one-size-fits-all reaction to every conflict. This is why we are designed to trust the Spirit, who is always faithful to guide us from the heart in every unique situation.

Thoughts on Marriage

Ephesians is one of the few places in the New Testament that talks about marriage. It specifically addresses the needs of husbands and wives. It likens the marriage relationship to Christ and the Church:

> *Wives, be subject to your own husbands, as to the Lord. For the husband is the head of the wife, as Christ also is the head of the church, He Himself being the Savior of the body. But as the church is subject to Christ, so also the wives ought to be to their husbands in everything.* (Ephesians 5:22–24)

A husband needs respect. Constantly nagging someone causes them to feel disrespected. Allowing them space to be who they are is key. Then they are more likely to return to interactions "recharged" and ready to give love to their wives. And love is exactly what Paul highlights as the wife's main need:

> *Husbands, love your wives, just as Christ also loved the church and gave Himself up for her. . . . So husbands ought also to love their own wives as their own bodies. He who loves his own wife loves himself; for no one ever hated his own flesh, but nourishes and cherishes it, just as Christ also does the church, because we are members of His body.* (Ephesians 5:25, 28–30)

A wife often needs her husband's loving presence, availability, and empathy. But it's difficult to listen when the temptation to "resolve" is always there. The husband can even be tempted to assume his spouse's feelings are his fault, and therefore he must fix them.

YOUR LOVING AND RESPECTFUL HEART

Since God is our Designer, He knows our design best. Through the Apostle Paul, God is telling us a wife's primary need is to be loved and cherished, and a husband's primary need is to be respected.

While our "head" may not realize this all the time, our heart is prepared in any moment to love and respect in this way. Think about it: If we already have everything we need for life and godliness, then God has already programmed within the new heart a desire to love and respect others in this way. In other words, God is not asking us to do something we don't already have written on our hearts. We have new and obedient hearts, and these longings to love and respect are already etched within.

The born-again wife wants to respect her husband, and the born-again husband wants to cherish his wife. We may not always perform this way, but our hearts are *always* longing to live this way.

This is why we need to learn to take the one-foot journey from head to heart in marriage. We can respond from the heart, not merely the head. The Holy Spirit who lives within our new-hearted, perfect self will teach us to listen and accept each other rather than always trying to "fix" or change each other.

CHAPTER 27

Offering unsolicited advice is one way we often try to "fix" another person. If someone is an adult—whether they be your son or daughter, a friend, a colleague, or a spouse, telling them how they could do better when they haven't asked can easily be perceived as rejection. Even if you—the one offering advice—truly want to help, it can be seen as labeling the other person as incapable or inept.

A CLASSIC EXAMPLE

Here's a classic example from the marriage relationship: "I wish you were more of the spiritual leader you're supposed to be," says a wife. Maybe she's trying to inspire her husband, but she deflates him. To the husband, she communicates rejection. He digs in his heels and shuns her attempts to improve him. Maybe she resents something about his lifestyle, or maybe she just wants to motivate him to be more "faithful." But he feels controlled and judged.

But the rejection and disapproval don't always take on a religious face. It can often relate to things around the house:

> *When are you going to mow the lawn? It looks really bad.*
> (He feels shame.)
> *Please take out the garbage. I've already asked you twice.*
> (He feels controlled.)
> *Why are you always up at the office? The kids need you.*
> (He feels guilt.)
> *You're going fishing again?*
> (He feels disapproved/accused.)

In each case, she's either trying to remind him, or to ask him for help, or to seek closeness. But he feels guilted, disapproved of, and controlled. Notice that in each statement above there is a hint (or more!) of shame rather than encouragement. ("It would be a huge help to me if...")

As a result, he feels attacked. He may defend himself (his anger is a cloak for his hurt) or retreat into silence as he bottles it all up. He turns on the TV and appears to zone out. Inside, he's either coping or replaying the conversation as resentment churns inside. She sees him sitting there and thinks, "He couldn't care less about me and my needs." They both fume.

MISUNDERSTANDINGS

But not everything she says is expressed in a *wrong* way. Often, she is just misinterpreted. She complains about how messy the house is, or how the neighborhood is so noisy, or how their finances are so fragile. She's exhausted or annoyed or fearful, and she's simply expressing herself—nothing more. She wants to share her thoughts and feelings about her present circumstances. She wants to feel heard and cherished, not "taught" or "fixed." She is looking for empathy, for understanding. She just wants someone to be with her during the struggle.

He interprets her words as meaning he doesn't earn enough to hire a housekeeper or to move them to a quieter neighborhood. She's frustrated about *externals*, but he takes it *internally*. He might end up offended and rejected, and she can't see why. He feels that it's his fault, and that he can never please her. He's trying to prove himself and provide for her. He wants to be needed and successful at meeting her expectations.

She doesn't even see her complaining as a threat to him. Nevertheless, the complaints cut deeply. He might even feel humiliated. She doesn't know she's doing it. He grows impatient with her and lashes out for no apparent reason because he feels criticized. She never saw it coming.

They're missing each other's new hearts.

We aren't saying all of the above behaviors or reactions are always fleshly. But ultimately, it's about trusting God and your new-hearted self in union with His Spirit to show you when and how to react.

CONFLICTS

In any conflict with another believer, remember that you already "agree" with each other on some level. Conflicts that arise—in one sense—can be said to be "smokescreens," because they don't reflect the unity you have together at the core level. Your new hearts are united. You love each other with a God-given love. You can assume the best about each other, trusting that both of you have a God-given goodness. If you realize this at the outset, any battle could lose its intensity. And you might resolve a matter more quickly.

We just diagnosed one conflict (in marriage) as an example, but the solution to any relationship conflict will always be the same: Trust Jesus and communicate from the new-hearted, perfect you. Yes, it really can be this simple.

As you believe your identity doesn't stem from your achievements, you grow less sensitive and take less offense at the help, the advice, and the requests of others. As you learn to accept others as God does, the fleshly desire to "fix" them is less often entertained. As you find your value in Jesus (and are no longer threatened by help or advice), your conflicts are disarmed. This is the essence of what it means to "humble yourself" (1 Peter 5:6).

When you understand you're the new-hearted and perfect self, your relationships with others can begin to flourish in astounding ways. Relationships become more about expressing the life of Jesus than trying to suck life from the other person.

Remember the words of the Lord Jesus, that He Himself said, "It is more blessed to give than to receive."
(Acts 20:35b)

NEW-HEARTED LOVE

As a new creation, you're designed to love others. That's who God made you at your core. You actually want and are fulfilled by opportunities to give love. But if you're giving out of guilt or pressure or resentment, that's not the way your new heart is designed to function.

God's love is freely given.

When a demand is placed on you, it can result in a sense of obligation over the short term and resentment and burnout in the long run. This is giving in a way that God never intended for you. Yes, there will be sacrificial giving, but if it's tied to "I sacrificed, therefore you should too," then it's not the way of the new heart.

Over time, some people grow in giving more. Others grow in saying "no" more and setting boundaries in order to discover how their new heart is *really* leading them. And we grow in learning to receive love, even when our feelings tell us we're not worthy.

The new heart listens. The new heart loves. The new heart respects. The new heart empathizes. The new heart trusts. The new heart gives without a "tit for tat" attitude of retribution or reprisal.

When you realize this about the new heart God gave you, relating to others is not as hard as you thought. It's all heart-wired within you. You actually want to love others in this way. So you can simply offer yourself to God: *Jesus, inspire me today to express You to [my friend or spouse or family member], to meet his/her needs. Use my eyes to love them, my hands to serve them, my ears to listen and make them feel heard, respected, and cherished.*

The imperatives in the New Testament are *descriptive*, not only prescriptive. They reveal the desires of your heart. That's why the instruction is so pure and direct. God never tells you to love the best you can. That would imply a heart that might not desire to love. Instead, the New Testament imperatives assume you have a willing and able heart that agrees perfectly with God.

Isn't that beautiful?

Ultimately, though, you need to remember that you are the creation, not the Creator. You cannot bear the burden of being someone else's "answer." Although you are used by God to meet their needs, Jesus is their real Answer.

Blaise Pascal once said that we have a God-shaped vacuum inside of us, and that hole can only be filled by Jesus Christ. In this book, we have shared that the hole (in your spiritual heart) has been filled. You're designed to look within—to the Creator Himself—to get your needs met. You're designed to worship the Creator, not the creation.

EXPRESSING YOUR NEEDS

As new creations, we ourselves have needs, and we can express them. But even our needs can be expressed with love toward others.

The Bible tells us that "love believes all things" (1 Corinthians 13:7), so we can express our needs while *believing in the other person to rise to the occasion and meet them.* This is better than what often takes place: expressing our needs while *not* believing they will come through.

This deflates the other person.

We can also *give up our right* to have this need met by them. In so doing, we release them from any debt they owe us. So we're expressing our need clearly to them, but we're doing two things as we express it: (1) communicating trust that they have a heart filled with desire to love us and (2) canceling any obligation/debt to come through.

Also, we can express our needs using "I/me" statements rather than accusatory "you" statements:

It would mean a lot to me if ...

I feel ...

I sense that I need this right now ...

This is much better than the "You never ..." or "You don't ..." or "I wish you would ..." kinds of statements that often find their way out of our mouths. After expressing our needs with an "I/me" statement, we can praise them when they've been attentive—not in a condescending way ("Thanks for finally listening to me!") but instead with another "I/me" statement like: *It feels so good to talk it through with you. Thank you!*

All too often, we communicate from the head, engage in arguments, and try to win at all costs. As a result, everybody loses. We cut into and hurt the other. We act as an attorney and judge, presenting the evidence, trying the case, and convicting the other person. A fleshly mindset generally seeks *to win* or *to escape*, while the new heart wants to navigate the issues and understand.

Again, it's not really about saying the exact words presented here. That would be turning language into law! These are only provided as examples. The key in all of this is remembering our newness in Jesus and trusting God's Spirit to season our communication with His love and grace.

You Want to Forgive

When someone hurts you, there's a choice you can make to process that pain, talk to God about it, and release them from what they owe you. Here's how to forgive someone who hurt you deeply:

It hurt me when ... (event). It made me feel ... (belittled, inadequate, abandoned, controlled, etc.). But I choose, as an act of my will—because I am a new-hearted and forgiving person in Christ—to forgive and release them from anything they owe me, even if they do it again.

Remember, forgiveness is not forgetting. Even though you genuinely forgive from the heart, you may still carry memories of the painful event for some time. Having these memories (or even "flashbacks") is no indication of whether you truly forgave or not.

And remember, too, that forgiveness is not progressive. Sometimes we hear people say, "I'm just not ready to forgive yet. I'm still working on it." But forgiveness is not progressive. It's a choice we make to release someone from what they "owe" us (an apology, better treatment, etc.) with no strings attached.

Forgiveness is a choice. Sometimes in counseling, someone may say, "I don't know if I've forgiven them or not." (That's like saying you don't know if you made your bed this morning.) Forgiveness is an event that takes place. We make the decision to forgive—as an act of our will—even in the face of feelings that conflict. Yes, we can live from the heart and forgive from the heart even when our emotions don't line up.

GROWING IN HIS GOODNESS

As you accept yourself fully the way God does, you start to accept those around you. You no longer seek to conform them to your own standard of what is acceptable or "right."

God is the one who made you new-hearted and perfect. As you grow in your knowledge of His perfect goodness, you more often reflect the new heart He has given you.

Your new heart is a heart that *accepts*, a heart that *loves*, a heart that *respects*, a heart that doesn't hold grudges but *forgives*—a heart just like God's.

This is who you are. This is *the perfect you.*

EPILOGUE

Wow! What an incredible journey we've shared together! Can you imagine any Gospel message better than the one our God has given us? It doesn't exist! This is Christianity at its best. And there is no "deeper message."

We never graduate from God's grace.

HOW IT ALL STARTS

If you've ever laid tile, you know how important it is to get the first one right. If you don't, *everything* is out of whack. Unfortunately, we have first-hand knowledge of this. Both of us can think of a time when we wished we had a do-over, because the first tile (yes, that corner tile) was not laid well.

When it comes to what you believe about God and yourself, laying a proper foundation in that first corner is even *more*
important!

> *For no man can lay a **foundation** other than the one which
> is laid, which is **Jesus Christ**.* (1 Corinthians 3:11)

> *So then you are no longer strangers and aliens, but you
> are fellow citizens with the saints, and are of God's
> household, having been built on the foundation of the
> apostles and prophets, **Christ Jesus Himself being the
> cornerstone**.* (Ephesians 2:19–20)

You're no longer a stranger to God. You're His child, a
saint. But you won't fully understand who you are unless you
look to *Jesus, your cornerstone.* He informs you in a way that
no one else can.

THE PRESSURE IS OFF

God's first message to you is one of love and acceptance
and safety.

This means the pressure is off. Even when it comes to
growing in your understanding of God's grace, you don't have
to "get it." It's already true, no matter what you might think
in one moment or the next.

You don't have to chase after a loftier experience either.
No, God's offer in the Gospel is not a Fourth of July encounter with Him—a big boom followed by picking up all the
trash the next morning. No, you can rest assured that it's

about *an enduring understanding* that transforms the way you see yourself and God.

EXPECT OPPOSITION

Expect opposition. Not everyone is a fan of this message. Many people attack it because they see nothing more than a generic and uninspiring grace. They imagine a license to sin—forgetting that they're sinning just fine without a license! They fail to see the "heart" of the message. The Gospel is more than forgiveness and Heaven. God infused you with righteousness and made you a slave to it. You're addicted to God's goodness. And when you put this radical exchange of identities together with forgiveness and grace, everything falls into place. It makes sense from every angle.

God is not naïve. When properly understood, "the gospel of the grace of God" (Acts 20:24) is His wisdom on display. Because of Jesus, you're right-hearted now. God initiated this core transformation within you, and it'll never be undone. He took out your stony heart and gave you a new one. So you can afford to be totally forgiven and totally accepted without condition. God's not afraid of what you might do or how you might turn out. He knows full well what He started in birthing your new-hearted self, and He will finish it with the renewing of your *mind*.

So go ahead and get to know your heart where Christ dwells. Live from there and thereby live from Him. It's a fully trustworthy way, because God is not asking a bad person to live "good." He's asking a new-hearted person to live from that heart. Big difference.

ALL OR NOTHING!

If you want the Gospel to be firing on all cylinders in your life, you're better off taking an all-or-nothing approach. This essentially means deciding just how "finished" you believe Christ's work really is. It's healthy for any believer to ask these questions:

Forgiveness: *How forgiven do I believe I am? Even of future sins? Didn't Jesus say it was "finished"? Doesn't Hebrews say my forgiveness is "once for all"? What choices can I make in my life to more fully celebrate my total forgiveness—past, present, and future—and not respond to the enemy's accusations of me?*

Freedom: *How free am I from the Law? Did Jesus free me from the Ten Commandments too? Do I believe Jesus living within my new heart is enough inspiration to keep me from lying, stealing, and committing adultery? How can I more fully celebrate the sufficiency of my union with Christ instead of looking to rules and restrictions?*

Identity: *How new am I in Christ? If I'm born of God, exactly what kind of person am I? What makes me tick? What do I crave at the core of my being? How am I different from the guy next door? If temptation comes from the flesh and a power called "sin"—then am I satisfied with that explanation enough to believe fully in "the perfect me"? What choices can I make to let my new-hearted self and my permanent bond with Jesus be seen by others?*

These questions are vital, as the answers both shock and liberate. The Gospel is always better than you think, and the truth always sets you free. So, don't let the memories in your head tell you who you are. Let your heart speak. Allow your mind to be renewed by what your heart and God's Word say about your true identity.

Guilty thoughts invite you to look to your past. Anxious thoughts invite you to look to an unknown future. God's thoughts invite you to look to the present where you live in union with Jesus—right here, right now.

Dependent by Design

We are new-hearted and wonderfully dependent by nature. We should embrace the beauty of our design. But the beauty only gets buried when we're inundated with messages of "do more" and "be more."

We are complete. We lack nothing. We have everything we need for life and godliness. We are blessed with every spiritual blessing. We are equipped. We are ready. We only choose to "let" it happen, as Jesus told us to "let your light shine before men" (Matthew 5:16).

We are receivers, not producers. We're primarily designed to take in and reflect the love of God. Yes, we need His counsel. But even more, we need His comfort. We need His love and affirmation even more than we need His instruction. Not every interaction with God is about teaching us a lesson. Sometimes He just wants to love us and remind us that we are safe with Him.

It's one thing to be *informed*; it's another thing to be *loved*. Our identity is not based on how much information we have from God. That leads to a "know-it-all" mentality and an identity centered on knowledge. No, our identity is based on how much we are loved by God. And once we realize how loved and how safe we really are, we begin to live like it.

HIS GREAT LOVE

Have you been seeking to show off your love for God instead of banking on His love for you? Paul's prayer was that you "may be able to comprehend with all the saints what is the breadth and length and height and depth, and *to know the love of Christ* which surpasses knowledge, that you may be filled up to all the fullness of God" (Ephesians 3:18–19).

Have you seen how giant God's love is for you? God throws a party over you every day. He delights in you. He celebrates you with shouts of joy (Zephaniah 3:17).

For you to disappoint God, He would have to have expectations for you. But God already saw every sin you'd ever commit, so you can't disappoint Him. He's never caught off guard when you fail. When Adam and Eve failed, His gut reaction was to clothe them in their shame. Likewise, His heart is always one of rescue toward you.

We live in a performance-based society with transactional love. If you get good grades, you get into a better-ranked university. If you do good work, you receive a promotion. If you perform well, you're affirmed by others. And when you fail, you reap the consequences—disapproval, even rejection. You have to hold up your end of the bargain on Planet Earth, or else.

But God invites you to accept the challenge to think differently about yourself. You're not on a performance treadmill with Him. There is no point system. You already have a perfect score, even before you begin your day. There's nothing to prove.

You don't have to hide who you are from God. He sees you, and He likes what He sees. Yes, He sees the flesh patterns that plague you. But you are not those, and He knows it. So you can be open and transparent about your struggles. You are *not* your struggles. You aren't defined by them. They don't tell you who you are. You're not a broken mess. You're made whole. You're not the sum total of what you've done. You're valued on an altogether different scale.

You're right and good because of your (new) birth, *not* your behavior. By nature, you are good-hearted and good-spirited. Even your soul and body are holy and acceptable to God. He is for you—all of you. There's nothing wrong with who you are.

So what would be different about your experience if you actually believed the truth about your new heart, your new self, and your intrinsic worth to Jesus? God's loving embrace of you (*all* of you!) is more than a belief. It's divine inspiration for every move you make.

REFLECTING HIS LOVE

Jesus told us we would do "greater things" than He did. Any rational person has to wonder what He meant! Did He mean miracles, healings, prophesying? We think He meant *love*.

This is why He heart-wired within us a love for each other and a connectedness with each other. Genuine love for others is now your gut response. Loving relationships are your agenda and your destiny. You're invited to feed these new passions and desires and find real purpose in reflecting God's divine love to others.

1 John tells us that the world will know we are believers by our love. If you're known by your love, what does that say about your design? Your identity? You are a "lover" by nature now. You only have to choose availability for your true purpose to be unleashed.

It helps to know your own heart. Imagine the effect when you also know your spouse's heart, your children's hearts, and the hearts of those around you. You begin to believe they are good and worthy of God's love—the love that dwells in you. You start to trust them. And when you can't, you release them to God.

Either way, you can recognize that you both share a mutual enemy—sin. You're not your own worst enemy, and neither are they. Sin is your common opponent. Understanding this inspires deeper relationships, as we can more fully be ourselves and give others the same freedom. We hold no agenda to manipulate and change, and instead we trust the process—a "growth that comes from God" (Colossians 2:19).

People pay attention when they're loved. It catches them by surprise. They notice, because it's unusual. *Agape* love may even come across as a little out of place, given the deprived world we live in. We have to be willing to be misunderstood in our love for others.

Ministry is love. Yes, we make too much out of the word. Ministry is nothing more than bearing fruit. We are all in ministry, and we're all qualified as ministers of the new covenant—just make sure that's what you're ministering! In so doing, you'll live with an incredible sense of purpose and meaning as you are enjoying and sharing the limitless love of God.

You—the perfect you—are accepting God's invitation to live from the heart.

RECEIVING A NEW HEART

God invites you to live from the heart, but only if you have the new heart given by Him.

Here's how that happens: When you hear and believe the message that Jesus died for your sins, and that He rose from the dead to give you new life, and you open the door of your life to Him, Jesus promises to come in and change you from the inside out.

If you've never accepted God's invitation to live new and free in Jesus, we encourage you to express your desire to God. He promises to respond and do an amazing and irreversible work within you!

> *Lord Jesus Christ, I believe I am a sinner in need of forgiveness and new life from You. I believe You are the Son of God who died on the cross to offer me forgiveness.*

*I believe You rose from the dead to give me new life.
Right now, I open the door of my life to You and receive
You so that You can transform me from the inside out.
In Your name, amen.*

If you prayed this prayer to accept Jesus Christ into your life, we'd love to hear from you. Send us your story at:

Andrew@AndrewFarley.org
Tim@GraceLifeFellowship.org

Study Questions

Part 1: In Search of Perfection

1. What popular religious messages of "do more" and "be more" have you heard in your circles?
2. Have you seen evidence of "cookie-cutter Christianity" that seeks to press everyone into the same mold?
3. In what ways have you been tempted to compare yourself with others? To find worth and value in stacking up to them?
4. What labels have others put on you? What do you believe God thinks about those labels?
5. How might knowing who you really are in Christ help you deal with the opinions of others?
6. In John 17, Jesus prayed for you to have the same closeness—the same loving bond—that He has with the Father. Do you think His prayer was answered? Why or why not?
7. Are you good? What factors play into your answer?

8. Have you ever heard a spiritual leader say that we all have "wicked hearts"? What was your reaction then? How about now?

PART 2: THE PERFECT HEART

1. When the Gospel was first explained to you, do you recall hearing anything about getting a new heart or becoming a new self?
2. If you're recreated in Christ for good works, what does that say about your design? And what does your design say about your desires?
3. What does it mean to you personally to be made "complete" in Christ and to have everything you need for life and godliness?
4. Have you been looking at reading the Bible and prayer as spiritual disciplines? Has reading this book given you a new perspective? If so, in what way?
5. React to this statement: *I've got it all up here in my head. I just need to get it down here in my heart.* Have you heard someone say this before? Has your view of the statement changed since then?
6. React to this statement: *I don't really want to sin.* Do you believe this is true? If not, why not? If so, then where do the sinful thoughts in your mind really come from?
7. If you actually believed (and remembered!) that you have an obedient heart and you're a "slave of righteousness," what would it do for you?

PART 3: THE PERFECT SELF

1. Have you thought of yourself as a "sinner" or a "saint" or both? Does the "saint" label seem justified to you? Why or why not?

2. React to this statement: *You are not the sum total of what you do.*

3. What does it mean to you to be "a fragrant aroma" to God (2 Corinthians 2:15)?

4. In what ways can you make the "one-foot journey" from head to heart to improve the way you respond to others?

5. Why is it so important to see your righteousness as not merely *imputed* but also *imparted* to you? Why do you think so many people resist this idea?

6. React to this statement: *God isn't faking Himself out by looking at you through Jesus glasses.*

7. How can the truth about your being "born of God" positively affect your view of your righteousness?

PART 4: THE PERFECT STORM

1. You already have new heartware, but you're still experiencing software updates. How does this analogy help you understand the ongoing battle within?

2. How do so many Christians misunderstand the source of temptation? (Hint: F-L-E-S-H versus S-E-L-F).

3. React to this statement: *The source of temptation is not you.*

4. We wrote about the importance of "playing the game" and not freezing up—always wondering if you committed a foul. Relate this to walking by the Spirit versus analyzing the flesh.

5. Why do you think we humans are very prone to examining ourselves and analyzing our motives? (Hint: Consider one of the trees in the Garden of Eden.)

6. We discussed two types of programming in the mind— one was broadcasting failures, labels, and accusations; the other was broadcasting mind-renewing truths about who God says you are. How easy is it for you to "change the channel"? What are the biggest challenges?

7. React to this statement: *Trusting Jesus is your new default setting.*

8. In Chapter 11, there's a diagram of your spirit, your soul, and your body. Does it help you to understand the core of your being versus the sinful "influencers" in your life? If so, in what ways?

PART 5: THE PERFECT FIT

1. What does it mean to you that "your soul is Heaven-ready"?

2. React to this statement: *There's nothing wrong with who you are.*

3. Many misinterpret learning and growing to mean that they are progressively getting "better" in God's eyes. How is this view inaccurate?

4. Have you ever heard the heresy that your body is evil? Well, it's not. Your body is not an obstacle to God. It's His instrument! In what ways does that encourage you to accept *all* of you just as God does?

5. Evaluate this idea: *It needs to be more of Him and less of me.*

6. Have you ever been taught that God is breaking you? Or that He is humbling you? Having read this section of the book, what are your thoughts on those ideas? Do you see the "humble yourself" approach as truly different? Why or why not?

7. How might the term "surrender" get misused and even abused in our understanding of relating to God?

8. Do you need to "deny yourself" and "die to self" and "die daily"? Why or why not?

PART 6: THE PERFECT ATMOSPHERE

1. Had you thought about the new covenant before reading this book? If so, what did it mean to you? What new thing(s) have you learned about it here?

2. When did the new covenant truly begin? Why is its true beginning such a big deal?

3. How does Jesus amplify the Law, exposing its true and impossible standards?

4. How do the new commands (*believe* and *love* as seen in 1 John 3:23) differ from having the Old Testament law written on your heart?

5. React to this statement: *You died to the Law in order to serve in the new way of the Spirit.*

6. Why do you think so many people see the Ten Commandments as an exception to our freedom from the Law when 2 Corinthians 3 calls them a "ministry of condemnation"?

7. React to this scriptural truth: "Apart from the Law sin is dead" (Romans 7:7–8).

8. How do those who opt for God's grace truly respect the Law more than anyone who "flirts" with the Law and cherrypicks from it?

9. How is the Law a tutor to lead people to Jesus?

10. Under the new covenant, why did God make a promise to Himself? How is this an "anchor" for us?

11. What Christian rules or principles do you think are just modern-day substitutes for Law-based living? How do they hinder us from letting Christ rule?

PART 7: THE PERFECT SACRIFICE

1. What is "once-for-all" forgiveness? How is it different from the "again-and-again" forgiveness in the Old Testament?

2. Old Testament priests would always stand up as they offered sacrifices, but Jesus sat down when He was finished. What significance does this hold?

3. Jesus is the Lamb of God who "takes away" (not covers) sins. Why is this such a big deal?

4. Have you always believed that even your *future* sins were already forgiven? Why or why not?
5. React to this statement: *God canceled your debt. You don't owe Him anything!*
6. How does the message of "once-for-all" forgiveness inspire bragging on Jesus? How might the message be poorly communicated with a focus only on what we don't have to do?
7. Why did Jesus present a conditional forgiveness in the Lord's Prayer in Matthew 6:14–15? Is this the forgiveness that you have today? Why or why not?
8. James 5:16 says to confess our sins to one another. Is this to get more forgiven by God? If not, then why do it?
9. 1 John 1:9 is often touted as the Christian's "bar of soap" for daily cleansing from God. Why is this an erroneous view? Why isn't there a formula for daily cleansing in any epistle?

PART 8: THE PERFECT PERSPECTIVE

1. Explain "the art of doing nothing" in your own words.
2. Have you ever found yourself trying to do any of these: (1) get closer to God, (2) seek forgiveness and cleansing, (3) monitor or fix your heart, or (4) feel or "experience" more in the Christian life? If so, how has reading this book helped you?
3. What sort of spiritual distractions or experience-chasing have you been exposed to as a Christian? Were you susceptible to it? Why or why not?
4. Have you ever been told to "appropriate" a spiritual truth? Did you understand what that meant? How did it go?
5. How is your "vertical" relationship with God different from your "horizontal" relationship with other people?
6. Have you ever heard that you can fall out of fellowship with God? Do you believe you can? Why or why not?

What's wrong with using human relationships (like your marriage or your parenting) to explain how God relates to us?

7. Why is it important to keep the two types of sanctification (*you* versus *your behavior*) separate and not conflate them into a "progressive sanctification" of you?

PART 9: THE PERFECT GOD

1. React to this statement: *You'll see God being only as good to you as you are to Him.* What's wrong with this tendency?

2. Our theology affects our psychology. Why is believing in the goodness of God so important to how we think of ourselves and others?

3. 9/11. Hurricane Katrina. Coronavirus. Are these instances of God's bringing judgment upon the world? Why or why not? (If not, where do they come from?)

4. Some people insist that God is causing everything. Otherwise, He is not truly sovereign, they claim. What are your thoughts? Can God be in control without actually controlling everyone (like puppets)? Is there a "bigger" view of God's sovereignty that we need to consider?

5. 2 Chronicles 7:14 is often cited during disasters or pandemics. It instructs Israel to pray, seek God's face, and turn from their wicked ways, and then God will "heal their land." Does this concept still apply to us today? Is God the author of disaster? Does the cross change anything? Explain.

6. Why might God seem so different in the Old Testament versus the New Testament? If God hasn't changed, then what has changed?

7. How does Jesus show us the heart of God?

8. What messages do we have to share with the world today? What does God think of them?

9. How does knowing the goodness of God allow us to develop communities of honesty, vulnerability, and security?

PART 10: LIVING AS THE PERFECT YOU

1. Have you been tempted to "fix" other people in your life? What do you see as the remedy for this?
2. In your relationships, how does recognizing sin as the common enemy enable you to more clearly see others' hearts?
3. What do you think it does for someone when you "let them be" and "give them space"? What sort of attitude can enable you to do this for them?
4. The flesh wants us to jump in and solve every problem for other people. When this happens, we end up frustrated, disillusioned, even burned out. Have you experienced this? Knowing what you know about your new self (which opposes the flesh), what's the answer?
5. You've probably read many times that a wife needs to be loved and cherished, and a husband needs to be respected and praised. But how does "the perfect you" perspective on your heart help you address these needs via God's grace rather than legalism?
6. 1 Corinthians 13 says that love "believes all things." How does the message of the new heart enable you to assume the best about another person, even in the midst of intense conversation or conflict?
7. After reading the section on how to forgive those who hurt you deeply, could you think of anyone who has hurt you? Did you decide to forgive? If not, would you consider rereading that portion and taking some time out to release those who hurt you from any debt they owe? (This is your heart's desire!)

A Scripture Guide

Here is an opportunity to further celebrate all that God says about the perfect you throughout the New Testament. Enjoy!

I've been given the right to be a child of God.	Jn. 1:12
I'm born again and can see the kingdom of God.	Jn. 3:3
I will not perish, and I have eternal life.	Jn. 3:16
I believe in Jesus, and I am not judged.	Jn. 3:18
I don't need to thirst for more of Jesus.	Jn. 4:14
I worship the Father in spirit and in truth.	Jn. 4:23–24
I will not come into judgment.	Jn. 5:24
I have passed out of death into life.	Jn. 5:24
I don't need to hunger or thirst for more.	Jn. 6:35
Jesus will never cast me out.	Jn. 6:37
Jesus will raise me up on the last day.	Jn. 6:40
From my inner being flows rivers of living water.	Jn. 7:38

I have the Light of life.	Jn. 8:12
I know the truth, and it makes me free.	Jn. 8:32
Jesus has made me free indeed.	Jn. 8:36
Jesus knows me, and I know Him.	Jn. 10:14
I know Jesus, and I follow His voice.	Jn. 10:27
No one will snatch me out of Jesus's hand.	Jn. 10:28
Jesus is my resurrection life. I will never die.	Jn. 11:25–26
I have become a child of light.	Jn. 12:36
The Helper will be with me forever.	Jn. 14:16
I am in Christ, and Christ is in me.	Jn. 14:20
The Holy Spirit will teach me all things.	Jn. 14:26
I am a branch abiding in the vine (Jesus).	Jn. 15:5
I am a friend of Jesus.	Jn. 15:15
The Holy Spirit discloses the things of Jesus to me.	Jn. 16:14
I am not of this world.	Jn. 17:16
I am in the Father and in the Son.	Jn. 17:21
I have received Christ's glory.	Jn. 17:22
God's love is in me.	Jn. 17:26
I have been baptized with the Holy Spirit.	Acts 1:5
I am Jesus's witness.	Acts 1:8
I called on the name of the Lord and was saved.	Acts 2:21
I received the gift of the Holy Spirit.	Acts 2:38
I believed, and I received forgiveness of sins.	Acts 10:43
I have turned from darkness to light.	Acts 26:18
I have received forgiveness and an inheritance.	Acts 26:18
I have been sanctified by faith in Jesus.	Acts 26:18
My sins are not taken into account.	Rom. 4:8
I have peace with God.	Rom. 5:1
The love of God was poured into my heart.	Rom. 5:5
I am saved from wrath through Jesus.	Rom. 5:9

I have been saved by Christ's life.	Rom. 5:10
I received an abundance of grace.	Rom. 5:17
I received the gift of righteousness.	Rom. 5:17
I reign in life through Jesus Christ.	Rom. 5:17
I have been made righteous.	Rom. 5:19
I have died to sin.	Rom. 6:2
I was crucified and buried with Christ.	Rom. 6:3–4
I was raised to newness of life in Him.	Rom. 6:4–5
My old self was crucified with Him.	Rom. 6:6
I died and was freed from sin.	Rom. 6:7
I am dead to sin and alive to God.	Rom. 6:10–11
I am not under law but under grace.	Rom. 6:14
I became obedient from the heart.	Rom. 6:17
I am a slave of righteousness.	Rom. 6:18
I have been freed from sin.	Rom. 6:22
I died to the Law.	Rom. 7:4
I have been joined to Jesus.	Rom. 7:4
I serve in the newness of the Spirit.	Rom. 7:6
There is now no condemnation for me.	Rom. 8:1
I've been set free from sin and death.	Rom. 8:2
The Law has been fulfilled in me.	Rom. 8:4
I can now walk by the Spirit.	Rom. 8:5
I can now set my mind on the Spirit.	Rom. 8:6
I am not in the flesh but in the Spirit.	Rom. 8:9
My spirit is alive because of righteousness.	Rom. 8:10
The Spirit of God lives in me.	Rom. 8:11
I am a child of God led by His Spirit.	Rom. 8:14
God is my "Daddy Father."	Rom. 8:15
God's Spirit testifies with my spirit.	Rom. 8:16
I am a fellow heir with Christ.	Rom. 8:17

My body is a living and holy sacrifice.	Rom. 12:1
God is renewing my mind.	Rom. 12:2
I have been sanctified in Christ.	1 Cor. 1:2
God called me into fellowship with Jesus.	1 Cor. 1:9
By God's doing, I am in Christ Jesus.	1 Cor. 1:30
I have the mind of Christ.	1 Cor. 2:16
I am a temple of God.	1 Cor. 3:16
I belong to Christ.	1 Cor. 3:23
I will judge the world and the angels.	1 Cor. 6:2–3
I was washed, sanctified, and justified.	1 Cor. 6:11
My body is a member of Christ.	1 Cor. 6:15, 19
I am one spirit with the Lord.	1 Cor. 6:17
I have been bought with a price.	1 Cor. 6:20
I love God, and I am known by Him.	1 Cor. 8:3
I am gifted exactly as God wants me to be.	1 Cor. 12:11
God comforts me in all my affliction.	2 Cor. 1:4
God placed His Spirit in my heart.	2 Cor. 1:22
I am a fragrance of Christ to God.	2 Cor. 2:15
My adequacy is from God.	2 Cor. 3:5
I am a minister of the new covenant.	2 Cor. 3:6
My inner man is being renewed.	2 Cor. 4:16
God gave me the Spirit as a pledge.	2 Cor. 5:5
I am a new creature.	2 Cor. 5:17
God reconciled me to Himself.	2 Cor. 5:18
God is not counting my sins against me.	2 Cor. 5:19
I have become the righteousness of God.	2 Cor. 5:21
God's power is perfected in my weakness.	2 Cor. 12:9
Jesus Christ is in me.	2 Cor. 13:5
God rescued me from this evil age.	Gal. 1:4
I have liberty in Christ Jesus.	Gal. 2:4

I am justified by faith in Christ Jesus.	Gal. 2:16
I died to the Law. I live for God now.	Gal. 2:19
I have been crucified with Christ.	Gal. 2:20
Christ lives in me. I live by faith in Him.	Gal. 2:20
I received the Spirit by hearing with faith.	Gal. 3:2-3
Christ redeemed me from the Law's curse.	Gal. 3:13
I received the promise of the Spirit.	Gal. 3:14
I am not under the Law as a tutor.	Gal. 3:25
I am a child of God through faith.	Gal. 3:26
I was baptized into Christ.	Gal. 3:27
I have been clothed with Christ.	Gal. 3:27
I belong to Christ.	Gal. 3:28
I was adopted as a child of God.	Gal. 4:5
God put the Spirit of His Son in my heart.	Gal. 4:6
I am a child and an heir through God.	Gal. 4:7
I am a child of promise.	Gal. 4:28
Christ set me free.	Gal. 5:1
I have been called to freedom.	Gal. 5:13
My desires agree with the Spirit.	Gal. 5:17
I'm led by the Spirit and am not under the Law.	Gal. 5:18
I live by the Spirit and can walk by the Spirit.	Gal. 5:25
I have been crucified to the world.	Gal. 6:14
I walk by the rule of the new creation.	Gal. 6:15–16
I have been blessed with every spiritual blessing.	Eph. 1:3
I am holy and blameless before God.	Eph. 1:4
God kindly adopted me as His child.	Eph. 1:5
God freely bestowed His grace on me.	Eph. 1:6
In Him, I have redemption and forgiveness.	Eph. 1:7
God lavished the riches of His grace on me.	Eph. 1:7–8
I have obtained an inheritance.	Eph. 1:11

I was sealed with the Holy Spirit of promise.	Eph. 1:13
The Spirit is a pledge of my inheritance.	Eph. 1:14
God loved me with His great love.	Eph. 2:4
God made me alive together with Christ.	Eph. 2:5
God raised me and seated me in heaven in Christ.	Eph. 2:6
I have the gift of salvation by grace through faith.	Eph. 2:8
I am God's workmanship created for good works.	Eph. 2:10
I have been brought near by the blood of Christ.	Eph. 2:13
I have access in the Spirit to the Father.	Eph. 2:18
I am a saint. I am of God's household.	Eph. 2:19
I have bold and confident access to God.	Eph. 3:12
God's power works within me.	Eph. 3:20
I have been called to a new walk.	Eph. 4:1
God's grace has been given to me.	Eph. 4:7
I am growing up in all aspects into Him.	Eph. 4:15
Christ grows me and builds me up in love.	Eph. 4:15–16
I laid aside the old self. I put on the new self.	Eph. 4:22–24
I have been sealed by the Holy Spirit forever.	Eph. 4:30
God has forgiven me in Christ.	Eph. 4:32
Christ loved me and gave Himself up for me.	Eph. 5:2
I am a child of Light.	Eph. 5:8
I am sanctified, cleansed, holy, and blameless.	Eph. 5:26–27
I love Jesus with an incorruptible (undying) love.	Eph. 6:24
God began a good work in me and will perfect it.	Phil. 1:6
For me to live is Christ and to die is gain.	Phil. 1:21
God causes me to want and to do as He desires.	Phil. 2:13
I am a blameless and innocent child of God.	Phil. 2:15
I put no confidence in the flesh.	Phil. 3:3
I have righteousness from God.	Phil. 3:9
I am perfect in Christ.	Phil. 3:15

My citizenship is in heaven.	Phil. 3:20
Christ strengthens me to endure all things.	Phil. 4:13
My God supplies all my needs.	Phil. 4:19
The Father qualified me to share in an inheritance.	Col. 1:12
God rescued me out of darkness.	Col. 1:13
God transferred me to the kingdom of Jesus.	Col. 1:13
I have redemption and forgiveness in Christ.	Col. 1:14
I have been reconciled in Christ's body.	Col. 1:22
I am holy and blameless before God.	Col. 1:22
Christ in me is my hope of glory.	Col. 1:27
God's power works mightily within me.	Col. 1:29
I am now being built up in Christ.	Col. 2:7
I have been made complete in Christ.	Col. 2:10
I was buried and raised with Christ.	Col. 2:12
God made me alive together with Christ.	Col. 2:13
God forgave me of all my sins.	Col. 2:13
God canceled my debt.	Col. 2:14
I died with Christ to the principles of this world.	Col. 2:20
Rules are of no value to me.	Col. 2:21–23
I have been raised up with Christ.	Col. 3:1
My life is hidden with Christ in God.	Col. 3:3
Christ is my life. I will appear with Him in glory.	Col. 3:4
I laid aside the old self with its evil practices.	Col. 3:9
I have put on the new self.	Col. 3:10
I am being renewed to a true knowledge of God.	Col. 3:10
I am chosen of God, holy and beloved.	Col. 3:12
God forgave me (past tense).	Col. 3:13
I will receive the reward of the inheritance.	Col. 3:24
Jesus has rescued me from the wrath to come.	1 Thess. 1:10
God called me into His own kingdom and glory.	1 Thess. 1:12

My heart will be without blame at Christ's return.	1 Thess. 3:13
God has called me for the purpose of purity.	1 Thess. 4:7
I am a child of light and a child of the day.	1 Thess. 5:5
I'll be complete and blameless at Christ's coming.	1 Thess. 5:23
God is faithful to me.	1 Thess. 5:24
I have been called through the Gospel.	2 Thess. 2:14
God has given me eternal comfort and hope.	2 Thess. 2:16
The Lord will protect me from the evil one.	2 Thess. 3:3
The Law is not made for me. I am righteous.	1 Tim. 1:9
Christ Jesus gave Himself as a ransom for me.	1 Tim. 2:6
God gave me a spirit of power and love and discipline.	2 Tim. 1:7
The Lord saved me and called me with a holy calling.	2 Tim. 1:9
The Holy Spirit dwells in me.	2 Tim. 1:13
If I am faithless, Christ still remains faithful to me.	2 Tim. 2:13
The Lord knows me, and I am His.	2 Tim. 2:19
The Lord will award me the crown of righteousness.	2 Tim. 4:8
God, who cannot lie, promised me eternal life.	Titus 1:2
I am pure, and all things are pure to me.	Titus 1:15
The grace of God teaches me to say "no" to sin.	Titus 2:11–12
God redeemed me and purified me for Himself.	Titus 2:14
God saved me, washed me, and renewed me.	Titus 3:5
God poured out the Holy Spirit upon me richly.	Titus 3:6
I've been justified and made an heir of eternal life.	Titus 3:7
God speaks to me in the message of Jesus.	Heb. 1:2
Jesus purified me of sin once and then sat down.	Heb. 1:3
Jesus is the author of my salvation.	Heb. 2:10
I am sanctified.	Heb. 2:11
Jesus and I have the same Father.	Heb. 2:11
Jesus is not ashamed to call me His sibling.	Heb. 2:11
Jesus comes to my aid when I am tempted.	Heb. 2:18

I am holy and a partaker of a heavenly calling.	Heb. 3:1
I am a partaker of Christ.	Heb. 3:14
I have believed and entered God's rest.	Heb. 4:3
I can draw near with confidence to God's throne.	Heb. 4:16
Jesus is my source of eternal salvation.	Heb. 5:9
Great things accompany my salvation.	Heb. 6:9
Two unchangeables (God and God) anchor my soul.	Heb. 6:18–19
Jesus entered the holy place as a forerunner for me.	Heb. 6:20
The Law is weak, useless, and set aside for me.	Heb. 7:18
I draw near to God through Jesus, my Priest.	Heb. 7:19
Jesus is my guarantee of a new and better covenant.	Heb. 7:22
Jesus saves me forever, because He always lives.	Heb. 7:25
God put His laws (desires) in my heart and mind.	Heb. 8:10
I know God intuitively now.	Heb. 8:11
God remembers my sins no more.	Heb. 8:12
The blood of Christ cleansed my conscience.	Heb. 9:14
I received the promise of the eternal inheritance.	Heb. 9:15
Christ suffered once to take away my sins forever.	Heb. 9:26
Christ will return to save me without reference to sin.	Heb. 9:28
I have been sanctified once for all.	Heb. 10:10
Christ sat down after offering one sacrifice for my sins.	Heb. 10:12
By one offering, Christ has perfected me for all time.	Heb. 10:14
The Holy Spirit remembers my sins no more.	Heb. 10:17
I am forgiven and don't need any more sacrifice.	Heb. 10:18
I confidently enter the holy place by Jesus's blood.	Heb. 10:19
I can draw near with a sincere heart and full assurance.	Heb. 10:22
The blood of the covenant sanctified me.	Heb. 10:29
I don't shrink back; I have faith and am preserved.	Heb. 10:39
I please God by faith.	Heb. 11:6
I have something better than Old Testament living.	Heb. 11:40

Jesus is the author and perfecter of my faith.	Heb. 12:2
I am disciplined for my good by my Father.	Heb. 12:7–11
It is good for my heart to be strengthened by grace.	Heb. 13:9
God equips me in every good thing to do His will.	Heb. 13:21
God works in me what is pleasing in His sight.	Heb. 13:21
I will receive the crown of life.	James 1:12
God's Word is implanted in me.	James 1:21
I believe God, and I am His friend.	James 2:23
I am righteous, and my prayer is effective.	James 5:16
I am born again to a living hope.	1 Pet. 1:3
I have an inheritance reserved in heaven.	1 Pet. 1:4
My salvation is protected by the power of God.	1 Pet. 1:5
My soul is saved.	1 Pet. 1:9
I am a child of obedience.	1 Pet. 1:14
I am redeemed by the blood of Jesus.	1 Pet. 1:18–19
My soul is pure, and I can love from the heart.	1 Pet. 1:22
I am born again of imperishable seed.	1 Pet. 1:23
I am part of a holy priesthood.	1 Pet. 2:5
I am God's own possession.	1 Pet. 2:9
I am an alien and a stranger in this world.	1 Pet. 2:11
I am free as a bondslave of God.	1 Pet. 2:16
I am precious in His sight.	1 Pet. 3:4
I have been given a special gift by God's grace.	1 Pet. 4:10
God cares about me.	1 Pet. 5:7
God is perfecting, confirming, and strengthening me.	1 Pet. 5:10
I am a partaker of the divine nature.	2 Pet. 1:4
I am purified from sins.	2 Pet. 1:9
I am called and chosen.	2 Pet. 1:10
I am cleansed from all unrighteousness.	1 Jn. 1:9
I have an Advocate with the Father.	1 Jn. 2:1
God's love is perfected in me.	1 Jn. 2:5

My sins are forgiven on account of His name.	1 Jn. 2:12
I have an anointing from God.	1 Jn. 2:20
The Holy Spirit is my Teacher.	1 Jn. 2:27
I am born of Him, and I am righteous.	1 Jn. 2:29
The Father loves me and calls me His child.	1 Jn. 3:1
I am born of God, and I practice righteousness.	1 Jn. 3:9
I have passed from death to life.	1 Jn. 3:14
I have God's Spirit, and I abide in Him.	1 Jn. 3:24
Greater is He who is in me than those in the world.	1 Jn. 4:4
I am from God.	1 Jn. 4:6
I love because I am born of God.	1 Jn. 4:7
I am loved by God, and I live through Him.	1 Jn. 4:9
God abides in me, and His love is perfected in me.	1 Jn. 4:12
I abide in Him, and He abides in me.	1 Jn. 4:13
I can have confidence in the day of judgment.	1 Jn. 4:17
I love because He first loved me.	1 Jn. 4:19
By faith in Him, I have overcome the world.	1 Jn. 5:4–5
I have eternal life, and that life is Jesus.	1 Jn. 5:11-12
God hears my prayers.	1 Jn. 5:14
The evil one cannot touch me.	1 Jn. 5:18
The truth abides in me forever.	2 Jn. 1:2
I have the Father and the Son.	2 Jn. 1:9
I am of God and a doer of good.	3 Jn. 1:11
I am kept for Jesus Christ.	Jude 1:1
I will stand before God, blameless with great joy.	Jude 1:24
I am a priest in God's kingdom.	Rev. 1:6
My name will never be erased from the book of life.	Rev. 3:5
I will sit with Jesus on His throne.	Rev. 3:21
I am called, chosen, and faithful.	Rev. 17:14
I am invited to the marriage supper of the Lamb.	Rev. 19:9
I will reign with Him forever.	Rev. 22:5

ENJOY OTHER BOOKS FROM ANDREW FARLEY:

The Naked Gospel
God without Religion
Heaven Is Now
The Art of Spiritual War
The Hurt & the Healer
(co-authored with Bart Millard of MercyMe)
Relaxing with God
Twisted Scripture

Follow Andrew Farley on social media:
Facebook *@DrAndrewFarley*
Twitter *@DrAndrewFarley*
Instagram *@DrAndrewFarley*

**Get daily encouragement from Andrew Farley
Ministries at:**
AndrewFarley.org